THE ILLUSTRATED ENCYCLOPEDIA OF
AQUARIUM FISH

THE ILLUSTRATED ENCYCLOPEDIA OF
AQUARIUM FISH

By Dr Stanislav Frank

CHARTWELL
BOOKS, INC.

PICTURE ACKNOWLEDGEMENTS

(Figures refer to numbers of illustrations)

1 Biegner B.: 121
2 Chlupaty P.: 323, 328, 329, 334, 335, 336, 369, 373, 374
3 Chvojka M.: 5, 15, 16, 18, 25, 27, 34, 35, 37, 45, 50, 52, 64, 65, 81, 83, 84, 100, 101, 107, 109, 111, 114, 115, 120, 122, 153, 157, 159, 168, 172, 174, 179, 183, 188, 189, 191, 192, 194, 247, 297, 298, 302, 325, 326, 327, 331, 337, 347, 348, 349, 351, 352, 353, 357, 358, 359, 360, 364, 370, 371, 375
4 Čihař J.: 22, 62, 324, 333, 340, 341, 344, 345, 346, 350, 354, 355, 361, 362, 365, 367, 372, 376, 379, 380, 389
5 Contardo P.: 93, 98, 113, 116, 229, 269, 343
6 Eliáš J.: 6, 11, 13, 30, 31, 41, 53, 67, 86, 95, 96, 103, 106, 130, 137, 138, 148, 149, 177, 190, 198, 216, 253, 254, 257, 258, 261, 262, 263, 289, 290, 295, 296, 311, 312
7 Frank S.: 1, 2, 3, 4, 7, 8, 9, 10, 14, 17, 19, 20, 24, 28, 29, 36, 38, 39, 40, 42, 43, 44, 46, 47, 48, 51, 54, 55, 56, 57, 58, 59, 60, 66, 73, 74, 75, 78, 79, 80, 82, 87, 88, 92, 99, 104, 105, 108, 119, 124, 125, 129, 134, 135, 136, 139, 140, 141, 145, 146, 150, 151, 152, 155, 156, 160, 161, 162, 165, 166, 167, 175, 176, 178, 182, 184, 185, 196, 197, 201, 204, 212, 213, 217, 222, 235, 236, 241, 251, 255, 259, 260, 264, 265, 274, 278, 279, 283, 284, 285, 294, 300, 308, 313, 317, 318, 321, 322, 330, 382, 383, 384, 385, 386, 387, 388, 390, 391, 392, 393
8 Franke H.−J.: 49
9 Hamřík P.: 32, 89
10 Korthaus E.: 338, 342, 363
11 Maták, J.: 316, 319, 320, 332, 339, 356, 366, 368, 378
12 Zahrádka K.: 163, 377, 381
13 Zukal R.: 12, 21, 23, 26, 33, 61, 63, 68, 69, 70, 71, 72, 76, 77, 85, 90, 91, 94, 97, 102, 110, 112, 117, 118, 123, 126, 127, 128, 131, 132, 133, 142, 143, 144, 147, 154, 158, 164, 169, 170, 171, 173, 180, 181, 186, 187, 193, 195, 199, 200, 202, 203, 205, 206, 207, 208, 209, 210, 211, 214, 215, 218, 219, 220, 221, 223, 224, 225, 226, 227, 228, 230, 231, 232, 233, 234, 237, 238, 239, 240, 242, 243, 244, 245, 246, 248, 249, 250, 252, 256, 266, 267, 268, 270, 271, 272, 273, 275, 276, 277, 280, 281, 282, 286, 287, 288, 291, 292, 293, 299, 301, 303, 304, 305, 306, 307, 309, 310, 314, 315

Photographs on p. 10 by J. Eliáš, on pp. 6 and 11 by M. Chvojka, on pp. 15, 17 and 18 by R. Zukal, microphotographs on pp. 19, 20 and 21 by S. Frank, on p. 18 by K. Zahrádka.
Line-drawings by S. Frank.

Text by Dr Stanislav Frank
Translated by Edwin Kovanda
Graphic design by Miroslav Barankiewicz

Published by
CHARTWELL BOOKS, INC.
A Division of BOOK SALES, INC.
110 Enterprise Avenue
Secaucus, New Jersey 07094

Produced by The Promotional Reprint
Company Limited, 1993.

ISBN 1 55521 879 2
Printed in Slovakia by SVORNOSŤ, Bratislava
3/11/06/51-03

CONTENTS

THE WORLD OF AQUARIUM FISH IN COLOUR

The word fish conjures up different images to different people. The sporting fisherman thinks of overpowering the largest catch, the scuba diver swims along intoxicated by mysterious underwater bushes and nooks of magnificent coral reefs, and the breeder of exotic fish is amazed at the display of colours and shapes of live fish in the aquarium. Many people, though deprived of such real experience are nevertheless enticed and attracted to the silent underwater kingdom which to terrestial creatures is almost inaccessible.

Fish have been an important part of man's diet and in many places of the world, especially in coastal regions, man lives almost exclusively on fish. Even in landlocked countries freshwater fish, inhabiting lakes and rivers, can be a considerable economic asset. Over the last one thousand years many ponds have been constructed for breeding fish for food or sport and there is a long history of nations keeping fish to please the human eye. China, for example, has a very long tradition of breeding goldfish.

Modern aquaristics originated in science laboratories during the mid—19th century and was soon taken up by amateur breeders. It is now a popular hobby all over the world and often goes beyond a pastime. Many aquarists become ichthyologists and taxonomists. They make interesting and stimulating ethological observations, carry out genetical experiments with cross-breeding fish and collect fish that live in the wild. Some pursue their hobby alone while others work in cooperation with different zoological or ichthyological institutions.

The most suitable fish species for aquarium breeding are those from tropical or subtropical regions. The fish remain very active throughout the year, do not require a winter rest period and are not dependent on seasonal or climatic changes. While the cool waters of the polar and temperate regions are inhabited by relatively few species, tropical and subtropical areas provide a suitable habitat for many small, colourful and often bizarrely shaped species. It is with the tropical fish that this book is concerned. The book does not give a strict systematic survey. Instead, fish species are grouped into chapters on the basis of similarities of environment or behaviour. However their evolutionary relationships are not completely ignored.

THE ORIGIN OF FISH

Fish are gill-breathing vertebrates which, with some exceptions, live permanently in water. They first appeared in the Silurian period (450 million to 430 million years ago) and by the Devonian and Carboniferous periods (420 million to 350 million years ago) were wide-spread and possibly, in terms of different species, the most numerous inhabitants of the planet. It is difficult to decipher the different evolutionary lines of living species as fossil evidence is poor. The Indian Ocean, which has the richest fish fauna, is often considered to be the centre of diversification. Palaeontological finds of ancient fossil fish in freshwater deposits, and geological theories concerning the formation of continents and oceans do not, however, support this theory. Fish could have originated in freshwater and only later inhabited the sea. Most ichthyologists are inclined today to believe that living species are partly of marine and partly of freshwater origin.

NUMBER OF SPECIES

The latest carefully researched estimate of the number of species currently living was made in 1970 by the American ichthyologist, D. M. Cohen. He estimated that there are about 50 species of Agnatha (jawless fishes), 515 to 555 species of Chondrichthyes (cartilaginous fishes) and 19,135 to 20,980 species of Osteichthyes (bony fishes). About 100 new species of fish are discovered and described every year.

Within the approximate number of 20,000 fish species there are:

Primary freshwater fish — 33.1 %
Secondary freshwater fish — 8.1 %
Alternating freshwater and sea fish (diadromous) — 0.6 %
Sea fish living in coastal warm water — 39.9 %
Sea fish living in coastal cold water — 5.6 %
Sea fish living at the sea bottom (benthic) — 6.4 %
Sea fish living far from the coast close to the water surface (epipelagic) — 1.3 %
Deep sea fish living at depths of more than 200 metres — about 5.0 %

Freshwater fish comprise about 41.2 % of all fish species. These inhabitants of streams, rivers and lakes are most exposed to the direct influence of man and it is highly significant that almost half of the living species are subject directly to considerable changes in the environment and are endangered by human activity.

PHYSICAL APPEARANCE OF FISH

The shape of a fish is adapted to its habitat and its mode of feeding. The ideal body, as seen in good swimmers, is torpedo-like (sharks or salmon), or slightly flattened from side to side (the genera *Serrasalmus, Thymallus).* Fish that catch their food on the water surface have straight backs (genera *Danio, Alburnus, Pelecus*); fish living close to the bottom have flat bellies (genera *Abramis, Silurus, Corydoras*). Very conspicuous flattening of the body as an adaptation to life on the bottom is a characteristic trait of mature skates (rays). Similar adaptation occurs in mature plaice which lie on their flattened left or right body-side.

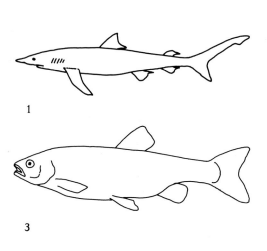

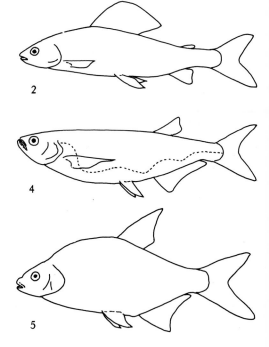

1. The torpedo shape of the shark *Prionace glauca*
2. The cylindrical shape of a chub *(Leuciscus cephalus)*
3. Cylindrical shape, slightly compressed on sides, in the Grayling *(Thymallus thymallus)*
4. The straight back of the Sichel *(Pelecus cultratus)* picking food on water surface

Fish that live permanently in slow flowing waters are greatly flattened from side to side, such as bream (genus *Abramis*), angelfish (genus *Pterophyllum*) and discus (genus *Symphysodon*). The bodies of some fish are conspicuously elongate and cylindrical such as mud fishes or loaches (family Cobitidae) and the egg-laying tooth-carps (family Cyprinodontidae), or snake-like, such as eels and morays. Others can be very narrow, such as garfishes (genus *Belone*) and halfbeaks (genus *Dermogenys*), or even needle-shaped, such as pipefishes (genus *Syngnathus, Nerophis*).

The body of a fish consists of a head, trunk and tail and each part merges smoothly into the other. The position of the mouth is related to feeding habits. Three main positions are distinguished; terminal, superior and inferior. The paired olfactory pits are elongate and tubular in some species and can be covered with a fold of skin which guides water onto the olfactory mucous membrane. The water then runs out of the pit behind. The olfactory pits are blind; they are not connected with the mouth and lie in front of the eyes. The lower jaw is usually bordered by a varying number of tactile barbels.

A fish's limbs are membranous fins supported by articulated bony rays. The rays are either soft and branched or hard and unbranched, and are often developed as spines or spikes, sometimes armed with a varying number of 'teeth'. Fins are either unpaired (dorsal, anal, caudal), or paired (pectoral, pelvic). Some fins can be absent, doubled or tripled (there may be several dorsal or anal fins). In some fish there is an additional fin on the back close to the tail known as the adipose fin, which is not supported by bony rays (salmonids, characins, catfishes) or has just one hard ray on the leading edge (the genus *Corydoras*). The pectoral fins can also be greatly enlarged enabling some fishes to fly (e. g. the genera *Exocoetus, Gasteropelecus, Pantodon*).

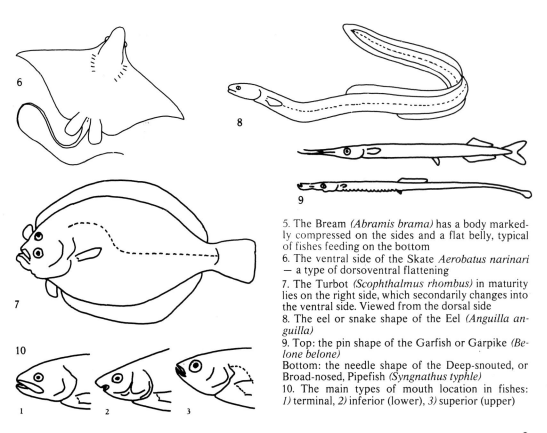

5. The Bream *(Abramis brama)* has a body markedly compressed on the sides and a flat belly, typical of fishes feeding on the bottom
6. The ventral side of the Skate *Aerobatus narinari* — a type of dorsoventral flattening
7. The Turbot *(Scophthalmus rhombus)* in maturity lies on the right side, which secondarily changes into the ventral side. Viewed from the dorsal side
8. The eel or snake shape of the Eel *(Anguilla anguilla)*
9. Top: the pin shape of the Garfish or Garpike *(Belone belone)*
Bottom: the needle shape of the Deep-snouted, or Broad-nosed, Pipefish *(Syngnathus typhle)*
10. The main types of mouth location in fishes: *1)* terminal, *2)* inferior (lower), *3)* superior (upper)

11. Tactile barbels and dermal tentacles, filaments and spines on the head of the South-American Catfish *Ancistrus multispinnis.*
Left: the ventral side. Right: the dorsal side

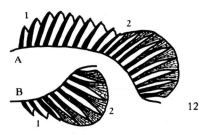

12. The hard (1) and soft (2) fin rays in the dorsal (A) and anal (B) fin on the perch-like fishes

13. The main types of fin: Top: in a salmon — the pectoral (A) and pelvic (B) fins are paired, the dorsal (C), caudal (D) and anal (E) unpaired. A small adipose fin (F) without fin rays is located between the dorsal and caudal fin
Centre: in a perch — a so-called hard (front) and soft (back) dorsal fin.
Bottom: fin type of mackerels. Multiplication of the dorsal and anal fins

14. Multiplication of the dorsal fins in the African Bichir *(Polypterus bichir)*

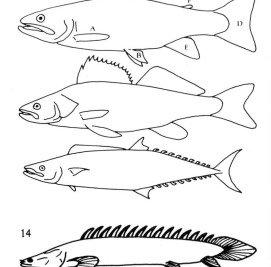

10

15. The body of the Flying Common Hatchetfish *(Gasteropelecus sternicla)*, heavily flattened on sides, with highly developed muscles of the pectoral fins

COLOURING

The colours of fish vary from silver-grey or grey-blue to very bright and patterned, and from translucent or white to dark brown and deep black. Colouring can be a sexual trait as well as a specific one. The males are usually more colourful than the females and in many tropical fish the colours of the sexes differ so greatly that males and females have been described as separate species. Sometimes the males become brilliantly coloured only during the breeding period.

Colour and body shape sometimes have a protective function and enable a fish to blend with its environment. Some seahorses and pipefish combine colour with filament-like projections from their bodies and so resemble sea algae.

The colour of a fish rarely remains unchanged. The pigmented cells, or chromatophores, are connected with nerve endings and this enables the fish to quickly change its colour and patterns. Plaice are a fine example; they change their colour and pattern to match the colour and simulate the structure of the seabed. In this way they become so perfectly camouflaged that it is very difficult to distinguish them from their surroundings. Many fish, such as species of *Poecilobrycon* and *Latris,* also change colour at night. Brighter colours generally disappear with age, when the fish usually turn dark and become less conspicuous.

16. The male American Bowfin *(Amia calva)* is more colourful than his consort

11

17. The day-time colouring of the Tube-mouthed Pencilfish, *Poecilobrycon (Nannobrycon) eques.* Top: male; bottom: female

18. The same pair of tube-mouthed pencilfish at night

SIZE AND AGE

Fish grow all their lives, but the rate of growth decreases as a fish ages. Generally, there are size limits for each species, and no individual can grow beyond them. The interspecific differences in size are considerable; there are giants such as the Whale Shark which can be more than 20 metres long. At the other end of the scale for instance, the mature male of *Pandaka pygmaea* is no longer than 7.5 mm, the male of *Mistichthys luzonensis* is 10 mm, *Microphilypnus ternetzi* and *Eviota nigriventris* 14 mm, *Neoheterandria elegans* 15 mm, *Poecilia minor* 17 mm, *Tyttobrycon hamatus* and *Grasseichthys gabonensis* 18 mm.

The life span of fish also varies greatly. The majority of species live a few years but some can live to be more than 100 years old. Some short-lived species, such as the small egg-laying tooth-carps (Cyprinodontidae) of Africa and South America live only for a few weeks.

BODY COVERING

In addition to their complex internal skeleton, most fish have an outer protective coat formed of scales of different thickness, structure and shape. The bony fish described in the main part of the book can be divided roughly into scaleless fish, scaled fish and fish armoured with bony plates of different shapes and sizes. The scales may be cycloid or ctenoid. The former are round and smooth, the latter toothed like a comb in the front, with fine denticles along the hind margin. Both types of scales are arranged on the body like tiles on a roof, the overlap being from front to back.

Scales grow throughout the fish's life by accretion at the margin. The increments form dense concentric annular rings. The darker rings are formed by many closely packed rings and these develop in winter or in periods of drought or lack of food. The lighter, or widely spaced rings, form in the summer or in periods of rain when the fish have enough food and grow more quickly.

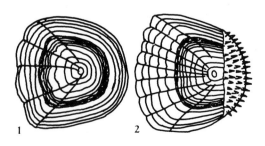

19. The main scale types of bony fishes: *1)* a cycloid scale, *2)* a ctenoid scale (on the right, small denticles cover the protruding caudal part of the scale). The thickening of the circles represents the first annual ring. The age of the scales of both types is less than two years.

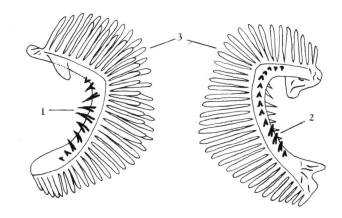

20. The first left gill arch of the Giant Danio *(Danio aequipinnatus)*. Left: front view of the arch; right: view from the back. 1 — the front series of gill filaments, 2 — the back series of gill filaments, 3 — the gill lamellae are the actual respiratory organs

RESPIRATION

Gills, the main respiratory organ of fish, are located behind the head and are supported by four gill arches. The front side of the gill arches is covered with gill tubercules (gillrakers) arranged in one or two rows. The gillrakers protect the actual respiratory organs (the lamellae and filaments) from damage and prevent them from becoming clogged. In some pelagic species such as herring they are used to filter food, particularly plankton, and to concentrate it in the mouth and throat.

In addition to gill respiration, some fish have accessory respiratory systems such as intestinal respiration or respiration through the oral mucosa or through a specialized labyrinth in the gill chamber. All accessory systems are adapted for breathing atmospheric oxygen, which reduces the dependence of fish on water and allows them to live in muddy waters with a low oxygen content. Fish which breathe intestinally, such as members of the family Callichthyidae, swallow air bubbles from which they absorb oxygen through a densely vascularized mucous membrane in a certain part of the gut. Mudskippers (family Periophthalmidae) absorb oxygen through the mucosa of the mouth. Another special respiratory organ is the labyrinth (family Anabantidae), a small chamber which protrudes from the upper part of the first gill arch into a suprabranchial cavity. The mucous membrane of the chamber is supplied with fine capillary vessels in which blood is enriched with the atmospheric oxygen from the air in the chamber. The fish breaks the surface of the water, takes a bubble of air into its mouth and exhales it under the gill covers. The use of accessory respiratory organs depends on the amount of oxygen in the water, on water temperature, and on the activity of the fish. The warmer and more deoxygenated the water and the higher the activity of the fish, the more frequently the fish has to surface.

In the lungfish (Dipnoi), the gills are underdeveloped and the swimbladder functions as a primitive lung. Other fish use the swimbladder mainly as a hydrostatic organ. In cyprinoids the swimbladder has two chambers and is permanently connected with the alimentary canal, whereas in perches the swimbladder is one-chambered and its connection with the alimentary canal is lost in the early stages of development. Regulation of the gas content of the swimbladder, and hence the buoyancy of the fish, is brought about by secretion or absorption of gas through the highly vascularized wall of the swimbladder. In some fish that are adapted to life on the bottom in running water the swimbladder is small, sometimes ossified, or completely absent (e. g. the genera *Steatocranus, Cottus, Acanthophthalmus, Characidium).*

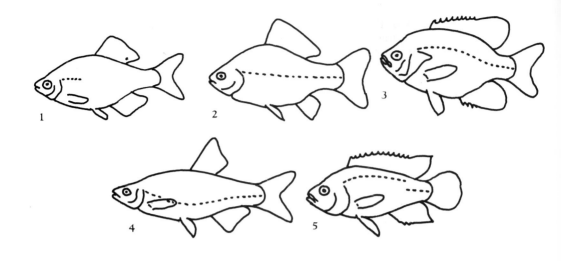

21. Types of lateral lines: *1* — incomplete, *2* — complete straight, *3* — complete, bent upwards, *4* — complete, bent downwards, *5* — V-shaped

THE LATERAL LINE

The lateral line organ of fish serves as a kind of fish radar. It is represented as a canal on the sides of the body and as a branching system of canals on the head. The canal runs through the separate scales and opens to the body surface through small pores. The sensory cells are located in groups inside the canal.

The lateral line can be of various patterns. It can be incomplete (running through just a few scales on the body side behind the head) or complete (running through the scales from the gill covers down to the tail). It can either be straight or arched upwards or downwards, or it can be split into two branches. With this radar the fish receives information about the distance and shape of neighbouring objects, and finds its way even in turbid water. The pattern of the lateral line is similar in all individuals of one species and the precise patterns may be used to determine the genetic relationships between many fish species. It is therefore a very important characteristic in taxonomic and phylogenetic studies.

ACOUSTIC ORGANS AND COMMUNICATION

It was once assumed that fish were dumb but they do produce a variety of sounds. Many aquarists know the sounds made by the South-American catfishes of the genera *Pimelodus* and *Platystoma*. These sounds are generated in the swimbladder where the walls are expanded and contracted by the lateral muscles. The mechanism which produces the chirping sound of the labyrinth fish *Trichopsis pumilus* and *T. vittatus* has not yet been conclusively explained. The fish are most vocal immediately before spawning, when they make a very sharp sound which is audible several metres from the aquarium. Individuals between 3 cms and 6 cms in length make the clearest sounds. The chirping sound is made mainly by the males and only exceptionally by the females. It is assumed that the sounds are generated by the movement of the gill covers and by the flow of air bubbles discharged through the gill cavity.

Besides the sounds clearly audible to the human ear, every movement of a fish is accompanied by characteristic low frequency vibrations. These vibrations are peculiar to each species, de-

SEXUAL DIMORPHISM

In many fish the males do not differ obviously from the females. However, an experienced aquarist can distinguish the sexes of most aquarium species by differences in behaviour, general habitus (the males are usually slimmer) and, in members of the carp family, by the so-called spawning rash. Male cichlids and labyrinth fishes are larger and more colourful than the females and the adult male cichlid has a large fatty cushion on its head which in some species disappears after spawning. In the mudfishes, the males and females have differently shaped paired fins. The males of egg-laying tooth-carps have elongate unpaired fins; the males of live-bearers not only differ from the females in size but their anal fin is transformed into a copulatory organ known as the gonopodium. The males of some catfishes have longer barbels. Their heads and sometimes their pectoral fins are covered with dermal papillae. In many species, particularly in the characins, the sexes are distinguished by the different shape of the swimbladder which is easily seen if the fish is viewed from the side against a light.

REPRODUCTION

Sexual reproduction with external fertilization prevails in the majority of fish. Internal fertilization is less frequent. Hermaphroditism is known only in a very small number of sea perches of the genera *Serranus, Lutjanus, Sparus,* and possibly also in *Sargus, Puntazzo, Pagellus* and *Boops.* Spawning may occur at one time or the eggs may be shed on several occasions. The sexual cycle is not constant; it depends mainly on ecological and climatic conditions. The number of eggs produced by spawning fish varies from year to year and depends on growth, age, weight, and on the amount and quality of food. These factors are well known to aquarists who study repeated

28. Examples of so-called phytophilous fishes which lay their eggs on plants. The picture shows a breeding pair of Schomburgk's Leaf-fish *(Polycentrus schomburgki).* The female on the left is turned upside down when laying eggs

29. An example of the so-called lithophilous fish, depositing their spawn on stones. The picture shows a pair of the Indian cichlids, Orange Chromides *(Etroplus maculatus)*

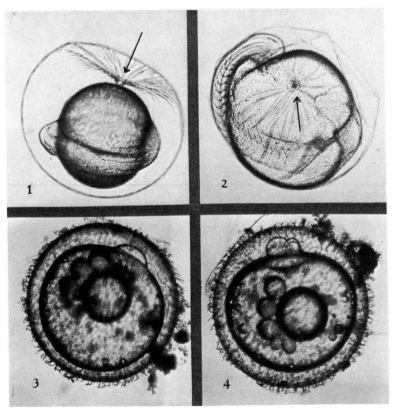

30. Figs. *1* and *2* represent different developmental stages of the Black Neon Tetra *(Hyphessobrycon herbertaxelrodi)*. The arrow points to the micropyle, i.e. the opening through which the spermatozoon penetrated into the egg. Figs. *3* and *4*: the beginning of cleavage in the eggs of the African toothcarp *Nothobranchius korthausae*. In *3* (top) the germinative disc shortly after fertilization consists of a single fertilized cell. *4* shows the cleavage of the right blastomere. The left cell is somewhat delayed in development. The surface of the egg case is covered with small anchors and filaments.

spawning of their parent-fish pairs. The fecundity is influenced not only by the age and size of the parent fish but also by environmental factors, particularly water temperature, oxygen content, salt content, age of the parents and infection by parasites.

In bony fish the egg is penetrated by only one spermatozoan through a small opening, the micropyle, in the egg membrane. Fertilization of one egg by more than one spermatozoan (polyspermy) is only known in sharks. In fish with external fertilization, the spermatozoa die in water within five minutes. However, spermatozoa which are introduced into female live-bearers through internal fertilization may remain alive for weeks or even months. One fertilization may be enough for the production of six or more broods of young without the presence of a male.

31.—33. Development of the eggs, embryos and larvae of the Cardinal Tetra *(Cheirodon axelrodi)* at a water temperature of 27° C:
1. and *2.* Two non-fertilized eggs *1* — about 1 h after leaving the body cavity of a female; *2* — about 4 h after spawning. Eggs, if not fertilized, soon become turbid and decompose, or are secondarily infested with moulds. The line section under Fig *2* = 1 mm; *3.* An egg about 10 min after fertilization. Telolecithal egg: top — the germinative disc consisting still of one cell, below — so-called nutritive yolk (deutoplasma). *4.* Germinative disc at the age of about 30 min consists of two cells (blastomeres) which developed as a result of the cleavage of the original single fertilized cell (zygote). *5.* About 45 min after fertilization the number of blastomeres has increased to four. The periblast space is clearly marked beneath them. *6.* At the age of 60 min the number of blastomeres is already twice as high (eight)

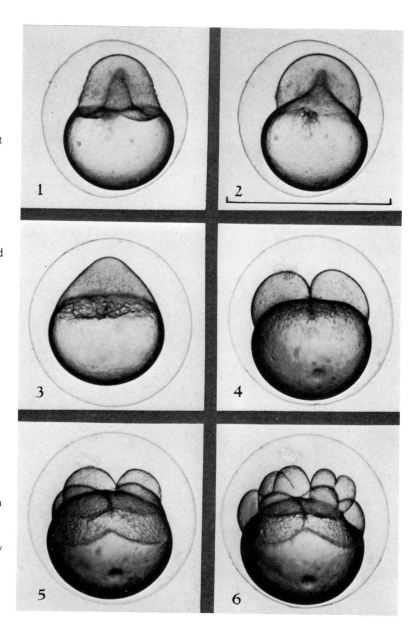

Fish seek suitable places for spawning after migration. Some fish lay their eggs in sand and others on living or dying plants to which the egg adheres. Other species stick the eggs to stones, roots, branches and other objects under water or just above the water surface. Some fish lay their eggs singly, others in a mass. The eggs may be heavier than water and sink to the bottom or, owing to a high fat content which makes them rise to the surface, lighter than water. In most cases the egg becomes very sticky immediately after fertilization and adheres to the substrate. Instead of sticky matter, the eggs of some fish have small filaments or tiny anchor-like projections which hold them on the substrate.

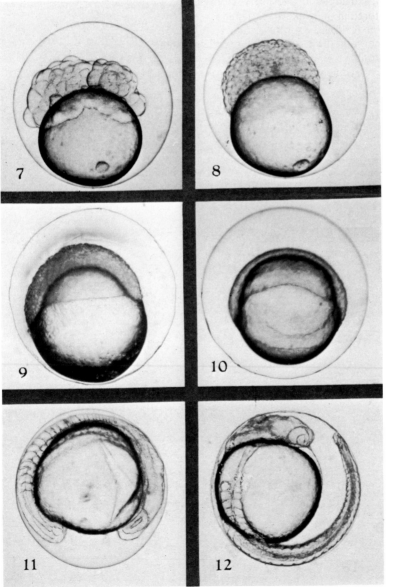

7. and 8. Cell size decreases more and more with further cleavage, producing the so-called discoblastula stage (7 — age 90 min, 8 — age 180 min). 9. At the age of 3 h and 30 min, the discoblastula changes into a discogastrula which gradually grows all around the nutritive yolk ball. 10. At the age of 4 h and 30 min, an embryo with a base of a head clearly develops on the yolk ball — (on the right side of the picture). 11. Further development of the embryo. The caudal part (right) begins to separate from the yolk sac. Age — 9 h and 30 min. 12. At the age of 14 h the embryo is fairly well-developed, in an advanced stage of organogenesis

DEVELOPMENT OF EGGS AND FISH EMBRYOS

The life of a fish, from egg fertilization to death, can be divided into five main characteristic periods: embryonic, larval, juvenile, adult, and senescent.

The embryonic and larval periods comprise the early phase and normal and healthy completion of this phase is vitally important for all the other periods of life. Knowledge of all these developmental stages should not be a matter of mere interest, but a necessity. An aquarist must know in detail the morphology of normally developing eggs, embryos and larvae and be able to spot and recognize any innate fault or defect caused by bad living conditions in the aquarium. A lack of this knowledge makes it difficult to create a better or optimal living environment which is necessary for healthy and productive fish culture.

The embryonic period, starting from the fertilization of the egg, is characterized by internal nutrition from the yolk stored in the yolk sac. It includes:
1. early development of the fertilized egg (the ovular stage)
2. development of the embryo in the egg case (the embryonic stage)
3. development of a free embryo with the yolk sac unconsumed after hatching (eleutherembryonic stage).

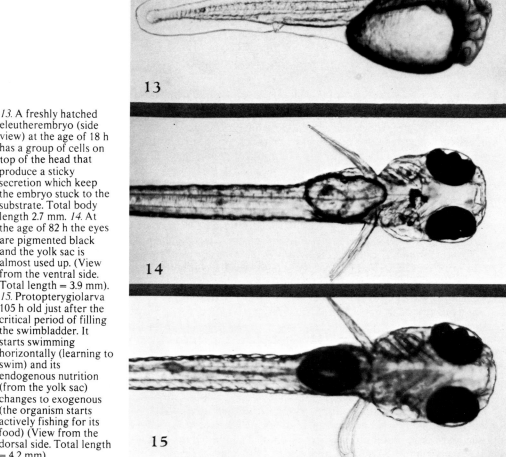

13

14

15

13. A freshly hatched eleutherembryo (side view) at the age of 18 h has a group of cells on top of the head that produce a sticky secretion which keep the embryo stuck to the substrate. Total body length 2.7 mm. *14.* At the age of 82 h the eyes are pigmented black and the yolk sac is almost used up. (View from the ventral side. Total length = 3.9 mm). *15.* Protopterygiolarva 105 h old just after the critical period of filling the swimbladder. It starts swimming horizontally (learning to swim) and its endogenous nutrition (from the yolk sac) changes to exogenous (the organism starts actively fishing for its food) (View from the dorsal side. Total length = 4.2 mm)

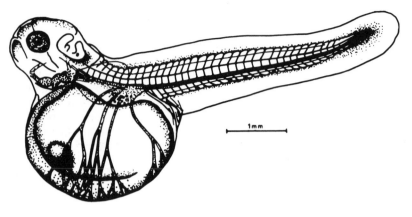

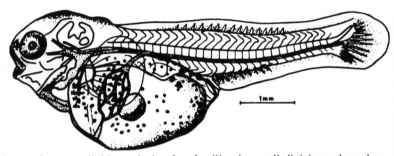

34. Miller's Thumb, or Bullhead *(Cottus gobio)*: Top: Eleutherembryo the second day after hatching with a huge yolk sac and uniform, undifferentiated, fin border.
Bottom: Eleutherembryo on the fifth day after hatching. The fin border has differentiated already before 'learning to swim'. The fin rays, forming the basis for the dorsal, caudal and anal fins can be distinctly recognized

The content of the fish egg does not divide entirely after fertilization; cell division takes place only in a small germinal disc (discoid cleavage). The disc is initially represented by one large fertilized cell (zygote), which subsequently divides into 2, 4, 8, 16 and more cells (blastomeres). These cells initially decrease in size and surround the lower and larger vegetative part of the egg which consists of the yolk for the embryo to live on. The cells gradually develop into an increasingly organized embryo which grows around the spherical nutritive yolk. The caudal part, coiled in the egg case, soon extends. Hatching occurs when the case breaks, releasing the embryo. The free embryo (eleutherembryo) depends initially on the yolk sac as the only source of nutrition. The embryo is attached to the substrate or to the walls of the aquarium by a sticky secretion (usually produced by glandulae on the head). Often it also adheres to the surface membrane of the water. The eleutherembryo remains inactive; indeed any unnecessary disturbance, such as vibrations or abrupt changes of light intensity, can be harmful.

As soon as the yolk is consumed, the eleutherembryo fills the swimbladder and enters the larval period of development. The fry 'learn to swim' and actively hunt for food. The larval period can be divided into two stages:
1. the body of the small fish is lined by a continuous fin border (rim) without fin rays (protopterygiolarval stage)
2. the fin border differentiates to form unpaired fins supported by the bony rays (pterygiolarval stage).

The larval period lasts until the skeleton is fully ossified and the embryonic fin border fully reduced. A number of temporary specific organs develop in the majority of fish during the larval period which act instead of the undeveloped definite organs. For example, the blood capillary vessels form a respiratory system on the gill covers and in the lower and upper fin borders of the tail. Further embryonic features include a blood capillary system which drains the yolk sac and carries food directly to the blood system, bypassing the gut; and sticky adhesive glands (byssus glands) developed on the top of the head or on other parts of the body.

FOOD

The mode of feeding and the composition of the food influence the overall organization of the body and have resulted in special adaptations, particularly in the position, formation and dentition of the mouth and the development of tactile barbels. In planktonivorous fishes, an important function is performed by the gill rakers on the anterior part of the gill arches. These form a dense filter for sieving all microscopic food from the water which is taken into the mouth when breathing.

According to the type of food they eat, fish can be divided into two major groups; predatory and non-predatory. The predators feed mainly on other fish but large crustaceans, molluscs, echinoderms and other aquatic organisms are frequently taken. The non-predators feed either on animal or plant food, or both. Irrespective of the kind of food, fish can be divided into those species which filter the animal or plant plankton (the planktonophages) and species feeding on the fauna and flora of the bottom (the benthophages). Only a few species live exclusively on the higher plants of the aquarium but some cichlids, such as representatives of the genera *Sarotherodon* and *Tilapia,* are an example.

When young, all fishes feed on plankton. From the aquarists' point of view, the wheel animalcules *(Rotaria),* the nauplius stage of cyclopses *(Cyclopidae)* and nauplii of the brine shrimp *(Artemia salina)* are the most important 'dust' food (very fine live food suitable for advanced fry). When they reach a certain size, the young fish start eating larger pieces of food such as adult cyclopses *(Cyclopidae),* water fleas *(Cladocera),* larvae of gnats such as *Culex* and *Chaoborus,* chironomid midges *(Chironomidae),* mayflies *(Ephemeroptera),* stone-flies *(Plecoptera),* caddis flies *(Trichoptera),* and even adults of swarming ants and termites.

Therefore some fish are omnivorous while others are highly specialized in what they eat. It is never possible to give aquarium fish the broad spectrum of food which is offered in nature. The main live food given to aquarium fish consists of *Cyclops, Daphnia* or tubificid worms *(Tubificidae).* This food is suitable and sufficient for the majority of tropical fish kept in captivity. However, some species do show certain nutritional difficulties during the reproductive season. This is probably due to the absence of hormonal components which are normally contained in the imagoes of insects which constitute the main component of fish food at certain times of the year.

Aquarists in large cities find it difficult to provide live food for fish. For a large part of the year the usual fish food is dry, artificial, frozen or even substitute food such as enchytraeids which are too fat. In recent years researchers and manufacturers have combined their efforts to develop many new kinds of high-quality, general-purpose and specialized artificial fish food. They have a long storage life which allows a continuous supply to the world aquarists' market.

At this point it is pertinent to offer some general advice for feeding. Administer food with care as the aquarium is small compared to natural conditions. For hygienic reasons it is advisable to feed the fish often (several times a day in the case of fry) but give them only as much food as they are able to pick and swallow in a few seconds. Thrift, not wastefulness, ought to be the main principle. Overfeeding can result in an excessive build up of organic matter and this can soon lead to calamity because of gradual accumulation of bacteria. This tends to increase water turbidity, oxygen starvation and suffocation and poisoning by waste organics (mostly nitrites, NO_2^-). The danger of overfeeding is greatest in winter when the light is poor. It is therefore advisable to prevent a calamity, rather than finally resort to the drastic step of partial or complete replacement of the water. The outcome of such a measure may not always be successful, for the fish may be too exhausted or the fresh water may intensify turbidity with the consequent increase of bacteria and infusorians.

ACCLIMATIZATION OF FISH IN THE AQUARIUM

Each fish species is the final link in the chain of antecedents in phylogenetic evolution. It is also a direct product of the environment in which it has developed, to which it is adapted and on which it depends. Both in the 'hardening' of fish and acclimatization of aquarium fish, success or failure depends mainly on the biological plasticity of the given species. The more 'stubborn' the imported species, the more specific its requirements (for instance, to a certain temperature or salt concentration) the more careful and sensitive treatment is needed.

Most aquarium fish come from tropical regions where they normally live in waters which are very poor in dissolved salts. Fresh water contains salts, mainly of calcium and magnesium, and these elements combine either with carbonic or sulphuric acid. In the former case, the compounds are carbonates and cause temporary hardness of water which can be removed by boiling. The compounds formed with sulphuric acid are sulphates and these cause non-carbonate hardness of water. This hardness cannot be eliminated by boiling. Throughout the world, the content of salts in water is measured either in millivals or, more commonly, in German, French, English or American degrees of hardness. This publication uses the German degrees. For conversion, see the table:

	mval/l	°Germ.	°French	°Engl.	°Amer.
1 millival/l	1.00	2.80	5.00	3.50	2.91
1° German	0.36	1.00	1.79	1.25	1.04
1° French	0.20	0.56	1.00	0.70	0.58
1° English	0.29	0.80	1.43	1.00	0.83
1° American	0.34	0.96	1.72	1.20	1.00

There are enough devices available on the market for quick and simple measurement of water hardness for aquaristic purposes. Titration has been simplified to the counting of drops or millilitres in a measuring cylinder until the solution shows a marked change in colour. Detailed instructions for use are always sold with these devices.

The main value measured directly is the general hardness (°dGH), that is, the amounts of carbonates and sulphates are determined jointly in the water sample.

Carbonate hardness (°dCH) is also measured directly. Non-carbonate hardness (°dNCH) is then determined indirectly as the difference between the two values measured.

With some exceptions (e. g. cichlids from the Malawi, Tanganyika and other lakes which are adapted to a high content of sodium carbonate), aquarium fish require low carbonate hardness. A high carbonate hardness may have an adverse effect on the development of eggs and fry. The amount of carbonates in the aquarium should be reduced to a minimum for both young and mature fish. The required hardness values, if known, are indicated in the text describing each species.

Water acidity (the free hydrogen H^+ to hydroxyl OH^- ion ratio in the water) is another factor which is important for the life of all aquatic organisms, including fish. The equilibrium state of the H^+ to OH^- ion ratio during dissociation of water molecules (H_2O) is expressed by pH value equal to 7. If hydrogen ions prevail, the pH is lower than 7, indicating that the water is acidic. However, if there are more hydroxyl ions the pH rises above 7 and such water is alkaline (basic). The scale is from 1 (extremely acid) to 14 (extremely alkaline).

The majority of tropical fish prefer slightly acid water, with pH ranging from 6 to neutral (pH = 7). pH is measured either electrometrically or colorimetrically. Small pocket pH meters for aquarists are manufactured commercially. However, it is often enough to measure the pH approximately (an accuracy within two tenths is sufficient) either by colour indicator papers or by so-called colorimeters with a paper or glass pH scale in a disc.

If care is taken to satisfy the water requirements of individual fish species then there is good reason to expect that they will acclimatize in the aquarium and successfully reproduce.

Chapter 1　　　**CHILDREN OF THE SUN**

Freshwaters of the tropical and subtropical regions of Africa, Central and South America are, as a rule, inhabited by large populations of colourful fish of the suborder Characinoidei which really deserve their name 'children of the sun'. They live in all waters of the rain forests from torrents to rivers and in savanna regions with shallow waters which are exposed to the sun. These fish are mostly very thermophilous and are subject to only small fluctuations of temperature (ranging mostly within 1 to 2°C) during the day and throughout the year. The optimum temperature for keeping them in captivity is about 25°C. The majority of them are lively, sociable and gregarious. For this reason they have become popular with aquarists throughout the world as valuable members of aquarium fish communities. Of the wide variety of families belonging to this suborder , only the representatives of the best known will be mentioned. These include the Characidae, Hemiodontidae, the hatchetfish *(Gasteropelecidae),* Alestidae, Lebiasinidae, Citharinidae, Serrasalmidae, and Characidiidae. A few characoids, such as some representatives of the family Serrasalmidae, are true predators; these are the vicious Black Piranha or the piraya which are among the most feared freshwater fish of South America.

Long-finned Characin (1, 2) lives in tropical West Africa from Sierra Leone down to the river
Brycinus longipinnis　　Congo. The males are larger than females and grow to 13 cm in length.
　　　　　　　　　　　Secondary sexual differences in the Long-finned Characin are pronounced and conspicuous. The male's body (1) is markedly elongate; the dorsal fin rays are frayed, the abdominal fins thread-like and the anal fin is arched with a whitish edge. In the females each fin is much shorter. (2 — bottom) and the anal fin margin is straight or slightly concave. The Long-finned Characin spawns for several months at two

1

2

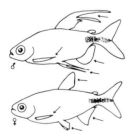

Brycinus longipinnis

to six day intervals in open waters near plants, stones, pieces of wood, or roots. Its eggs are 2.5 mm across. The incubation time is approximately six days and the temperature of the water should be 26—28°C. Immediately after hatching the fry start filling their swimbladders and their nutrition changes from endogenous to exogenous. At first the freshly hatched fish swim upwards at an angle of 30—40°. Their larval size is 7.2 mm. Only soft water (not exceeding 3° dGH of total hardness) is suitable for them in aquarium fish culture. It is advisable to encourage the development of these fish by adding five to six drops of ToruMin for every four to five litres of water. Freshly hatched nauplii of the brine shrimps *(Artemia salina)* are suitable for the first food. Adult individuals feed mainly on flying insects. This food is hard to substitute in the aquarium; the banana flies of the genus *Drosophila* can be used as a suitable replacement.

At hatching time the water in the reservoir should be intensely aerated, since it is easier for the young fish to abandon the egg case in water with an abundant supply of oxygen.

Congo Tetra (3) occurs only in the Congo basin in Africa. The males are larger than the females
Phenacogrammus   and grow up more than 12 cm long. The central rays of the caudal fin
interruptus   of the male (3 — top) are elongate and form a lobe which is much longer than the fin itself. This beautiful characin varies in shape and colour. It spawns mostly in open waters on sunny days. The large eggs are light brown in colour and do not stick. When laid, they slowly fall to the bottom. The fry hatch at 26—27°C within six to seven days, and their further development is similar to that of the Long-finned Characin. The Congo Tetra is a very popular species easy to keep, but it does not spawn easily.

Arnold's Red-eyed Characin (4) is found in the tropical waters of west Africa. It has a spindle-shaped body about 7 cm in length. In this species the anal fin of the males (4) is convex while that of the females is concave. Breeding and rearing are the same as in the Long-finned Characin but the eggs are much smaller (about 1.2 mm across). Rolf Beck has observed that the embryos hatch very quickly (within 30—36 hours) and are underdeveloped. They begin to swim after seven days. At first the fry are very shy. They grow quickly and at the age of 14 days they are 15 mm long.

Arnoldichthys
spilopterus

Black-line Tetra or **Scholze's Tetra** (5) is known to live in the Para basin in South America. Adults are about 5 cm long. The male is slimmer than the female. This characin has no special requirements and reproduces readily at a temperature as low as 23°C. Their reproductive capacity is outstanding; up to 1,600 young fish can be obtained from one spawning. Large glass spawning reservoirs are needed to keep the water pure when rearing

Hyphessobrycon
scholzei

5

so many young. In aquaria they will eat dry, artificial or plant food as readily as live food.

Serpae Tetra (6, 7) is a native of the Amazon and Río Guaporé basins. It grows to a length of *Hyphessobrycon serpae* about 5 cm. This species is closely related to the Jewel Tetra *(Hyphessobrycon callistus)* from which it differs in the bright red, lighter and more pronounced colour of the body and fins, and in a spot behind the gill-covers. This mark is normally small and square and may be missing in some bright red aquarium populations of the species. In *Hyphessobrycon callistus* the mark is wedge-shaped. The Serpae Tetra is easy to keep and rear and needs practically the same treatment as *Hyphessobrycon ornatus,* which is described below. The only difference is the short life span of the Serpae Tetra which rarely lives longer than two years in captivity. It often suffers from infectious dropsy which is practically impossible to treat and soon kills the fish. Young Serpae Tetra

6

7

8

readily reproduce throughout the year. They spawn over or near fine-leaved plants.

Pink Jewelled Tetra (8), which comes from the lower reaches of the Amazon and from the waters of Guyana, grows to 4—6 cm long. This sturdy characin is a good fish for common tanks. Excessively soft water is not recommended for keeping this species; it prefers water with a low carbonate content since the embryos are very sensitive to the presence of carbonates. Non-carbonate hardness should be no higher than 6° dNCH and the optimum pH should range about the neutral value. In water without hardness or in excessively acid water, many embryos suffer from constitutional dropsy; they fail to fill the swimbladder properly and do not start swimming. *Hyphessobrycon ornatus* is a very productive species, often giving five to six hundred young from one spawning. Advanced fry are fairly voracious and readily eat and quickly grow on the nauplii of brine shrimps. To avoid death of the young during the first three weeks make certain the temperature does not drop below 27° C. The young fish are highly sensitive to increased nitrite content in the water. It is therefore necessary to remove the detritus regularly from the bottom and to add fresh water of required temperature. Losses can be also avoided by timely transfer of the young fish to a swimming reservoir (a long, low and large container) with intensive aeration.

Sometimes the parent pairs refuse to spawn, or the first spawning

Hyphessobrycon
ornatus

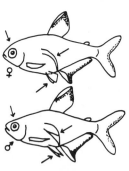

Hyphessobrycon pulchripinnis

30

yields just a few fertilized eggs. Such parents should not be replaced immediately but should be introduced again into the spawning aquarium after 14—17 days. Only the second spawning will show whether the two fish are fertile or not. Successful second spawning indicates that the initial failure was due to the over-ripened eggs of the female and that the two fish can make a good breeding pair. However, sometimes the male may be infertile and in this case must be replaced. The male initiates spawning by luring the female over a cluster of plants (such as *Fontinalis* and *Vesicularia*); then he presses closely to her side, and after an abrupt jerk a small cloud of slightly sticky brownish eggs falls

9

slowly to the bottom. The fry hatch at 27°C within 24—36 hours and start swimming after about five days. They will hide in plants for two or three weeks until they overcome their natural shyness. Then a small shoal of young fish appears in open water.

Lemon Tetra (9) *Hyphessobrycon pulchripinnis* also comes from Latin America, but nothing certain is known about how widespread it is. In captivity it grows to the length of about 5 cm. The male is more robust, but slimmer, and the yellow-black colour of his fins is more pronounced. This beautiful, calm and popular characin has similar aquarium requirements as *Hyphessobrycon ornatus*. The only difference is that the Lemon Tetra is less sensitive to lower temperatures. The fry tolerate temperature fluctuations between 24 and 26°C without problems.

10

11

Peruvian Tetra (10) is a native of the upper reaches of the rivers of the Amazon basin in Peru,
Hyphessobrycon   in tne neighbourhood of Iquitos. This small, finely coloured fish is no
peruvianus   longer than 4 cm when adult. It is much sought after by aquarists but
unfortunately only individual specimens are imported, usually together
with other species which are offered in large lots. All attempts to reproduce it in captivity have so far been unsuccessful.

Flame Tetra or **Red Tetra from Rio** (11—12) inhabits the fresh waters around Rio de Janeiro.
Hyphessobrycon   In aquariums it requires no special treatment. It is resistant and lively,
flammeus   and prefers the middle layers of water. The male (12 below) is slimmer,
with a blood red body and fins and black edge along the anal fin. The
body colours of the female are not so conspicuous. The Flame Tetra
tolerates winter temperatures as low as 16°C. It is an excellent component of mixed aquarium communities. The fish will spawn in glass con-
tainers with a loosely floating tuft of plants, or larger framed aquariums with standard equipment and a sandy bottom. They spawn both in
pairs (11) and in shoals in the proximity of fine-leaved plants such as
Myriophyllum and *Fontinalis.* The fry hatch from translucent eggs at
water temperatures from 20 to 24°C within 24—36 hours. They hang

12

on plants and aquarium walls until they start swimming (after five days). Flame Tetra fry readily consume not only all kinds of live food of adequate size, but also artificial feeds. However, artificial feed must be moistened before use to make it fall to the bottom, because the young fish do not pick their food on the surface.

Griem's Tetra (13) is a close relative of the Flame Tetra and Yellow Tetra. It comes from
Hyphessobrycon Brazil, near Goyaz. This lively, gregarious fish grows to 4 cm in length.
griemi When excited, it takes on a red colour. The breeding practices are the same as in the Flame Tetra, but the temperature should never drop below 20°C and for successful development of the eggs and fry, softer water is needed (up to 7° dGH) with a pH of 7.

Flag Tetra (14) is a nimble, gregarious, and peaceful fish from the lower reaches of the Amazon
Hyphessobrycon and Río Tocantins. It grows to a length of 5 cm. The breeding and
heterorhabdus rearing requirements of this species in captivity are similar to those of
the Flame Tetra. The Flag Tetra endures temperatures as low as 20° C.
If the eggs and fry are to prosper they should be kept in slightly acid
and very soft water (about 3° dNCH) with an admixture of peat extract. The optimum water temperature for spawning and rearing of the
fry is 26° C. Young fish eat only live 'powder' food.

Black Neon Tetra (15) is a native of Río Taquary in the Mato Grosso region, Brazil. It grows to
Hyphessobrycon 3.5 cm long. It lives in shoals in aquariums in the middle and upper
herbertaxelrodi water layers in places with aquatic vegetation. However, in aquariums
with poor vegetation, or with a light bottom, this characin feels discon-
tented and the normally showy colours are faint. All-glass tanks with

15

soft water (up to 4° dNCH) without carbonate hardness and with
a weak acid reaction (pH=6) provide the best environment for breeding this species. The male pursues the female along the aquarium walls
for a short time before spawning; then the pair spawn in mid water,
usually in the corners of the tank. The fish do not seek plants for
spawning and very rarely spawn in the proximity of aquatic vegetation.
In each act of spawning the female ejects four to six eggs which are
immediately fertilized by the male. At a water temperature of 24°C,
eleutherembryos hatch within 20 hours and spend a day lying on the
tank bottom. In the following days they hang attached to the walls and
on the fifth day they start swimming. At three to four weeks they are 15
to 20 mm long and their colour is the same as that of the parent fish.

Georgetta's Tetra (16)
*Hyphessobrycon
georgettae*

lives in the waters of Surinam near the Brazilian border. It is yellow to
deep red. The male is smaller and slimmer than the female. This characin is shy and pale if kept with other fish. In shops, where the fish are

16

always disturbed by frequent netting, they are similarly unattractive. They try frantically to escape from the net and throw themselves against the aquarium walls. The fish are usually small, about 2.5 cm long. They require a large, at least a 10—litre, all-glass spawning tank. The pair will soon quieten down to spawn in a tuft of plants after 1—2 days. The eggs of this small fish are relatively large and they are often laid in batches of more than a 100. At temperatures between 25 and 28°C the fry hatch after 18—24 hours. Live 'powder' food suffices to feed the fry in the rearing period. The young grow quickly and at 17 days of age they have acquired the same body colours as the adults. At the age of four months they reach sexual maturity.

If *Hyphessobrycon georgettae* is kept together with other characins in old aquarium water, it is susceptible to some diseases such as micro-sporidiasis *(Plistophora hyphessobryconis)* and infectious dropsy. In monoculture, the fishes are splendid and nimble. Frequent cleaning of the tank and partial water replacement are recommended.

37

17

18

Tetra Perez or **Bleeding Heart Tetra** (17, 18) is better known to aquarists as *H. rubrostigma*. It
Hyphessobrycon comes from Colombia and grows to 10—12 cm long. This beautiful and
erythrostigma decorative characin lives for a fairly long time. The male (18) is distinguished by its high, crescent-shaped dorsal fin. Information on the
breeding of this species is scarce. The behaviour of the male in attract-
ing the female (17) is similar to *H. ornatus*. Tetra Perez needs higher
temperatures, at least 25—26°C, and varied food, particularly flying
insects and larvae of chironomid midges, as well as artificial feeds such
as 'TetraMin'. The imported specimens are usually severely infected
with moulds. As they are very sensitive to any therapeutic chemicals,
the treatment should be based on increased water temperature in the
aquarium and frequent addition of fresh water. Fully mature males
look stately when swimming around each other with their fins widely
outstretched, a behaviour they often display for several hours.

Head-and-tail-light Fish or **Beaconfish** (19) is native to the Amazon basin and Guyana. It
Hemigrammus was imported to Europe as recently as 1960. Although it multiplied
ocellifer ocellifer very quickly, it soon fell into oblivion again. Since 1910, aquarists have
confused the Beaconfish and its subspecies, *H. ocellifer falsus*.

20

False Head-and-tail-light Fish (20, 21) is a characin originally living in the waters of Guyana
Hemigrammus and in the rivers and brooks of the Amazon basin. It is smaller than the
ocellifer falsus true Beaconfish and grows to a length of 4 cm. Gregarious and lively, it
is suitable for mixed aquariums. The fish are easy to breed and their
productivity is high. Water temperature should be kept above 20°C.
The milt and eggs are sensitive to higher carbonate hardness but non-
carbonate hardness may be relatively high (6—8° dNCH) in spawning
water. The adult specimens can tolerate general water hardness of
15—20° dGH with the pH being neutral or weakly alkaline. The breeding fish stay very close to plants when spawning (21). It is easy to rear
great numbers of fry.

Green Neon (22) was first seen and caught in the January Lake near the city of Manaos, Brazil.
Hemigrammus Later it was also found to live in the upper reaches of the Amazon
hyanuary from Iquitos to São Paulo de Olivenca. The adult is 4 cm long, the
female being larger than the male. When fished with a small net in the
aquarium, the fish try hard to escape, bumping their heads against the
aquarium walls or burying themselves in the sandy bottom. Their spawn-

21

22

ing is also lively and usually takes place at dusk. The fry hatch within about 24 hours at water temperatures of 24—26°C. Frequent partial replacement of water and removal of turbidity is vitally important for the health and quick growth of the fry.

Pretty Tetra or **Garnet Tetra** (23) lives in the Peruvian part of the Amazon near Iquitos. It is *Hemigrammus pulcher* a quiet gregarious fish about 5 cm long. For successful breeding a large glass tank is necessary (30—50 litres) because spawning is very vigorous. It is recommended to use only females with fully ripe eggs for spawning, otherwise the male may kill her in a short time. The pair of fish spawns in open waters, usually close to the water surface. The parent fish take no care of the tiny, translucent eggs which sink to the bottom. The eggs prosper best in very soft water (rain, snow, or distilled water with a very small admixture of tapwater). The water should be slightly acid. The number of young ranges from 400 to 600.

41

Buenos Aires Tetra (24) is a native of the River Plate basin. It is about 10 cm long. Because it is
Hemigrammus
caudovittatus
easy to breed it is recommended as a good species for beginners. The Buenos Aires Tetra tolerates temperatures down to 16°C. It is very voracious throughout its life. It feeds on common planktonic organisms (water fleas, *Cyclops*) and inhabitants of the bottom, (tubificid worms, larvae of chironomid midges) and artificial foods. It will bite aquarium plants and eat lettuce leaves, if offered. Neither the eggs nor the fry have any special requirements for water composition. They prosper in medium-hard tapwater.

Glow-light Tetra (25, 26) comes from Guyana and the female, which is larger than the male,
Hemigrammus
erythrozonus
grows to 4.5 cm long. A small all-glass tank with water hardness up to 8° dNCH will suffice for breeding. Although large quantities of fry will incubate in waters of low hardness, most of the fry soon contract non-infectious, constitutional dropsy, and die within a short time. Carbonate hardness should not be higher than 1° dCH. The addition of a small

amount of peat extract encourages the eggs to hatch. Water temperature should be kept between 26 and 28°C. The breeding pair spawns in a thicket of fine-leaved plants (26) such as *Fontinalis* and *Vesicularia dubyana.* At the end of each spawning act, both fish turn upside down and the female ejects the eggs in this position. Sediment should always be removed and new water added during rearing in order to avoid an accumulation of nitrites which can be toxic to the fry. At first the young fishes are yellowish but later they develop a dark pattern all over the body. They consume relatively large pieces of live food such as nauplii of brine shrimp. They grow well and fast.

26

27

Silver-tipped Tetra (27) comes from the waters of south-east Brazil and grows to about 5 cm
Hasemania nana   long. The female is yellow to olive green. The male is more slender and
larger and is beautifully copper coloured. The body colouring of these
fish varies a lot, depending on the origin and mood of the fish. The
parent pair spawn in the evening under artificial light. When spawning,
the fish squeeze their way through a dense tangle of aquatic plants. The
eggs are small, about 1 mm across, very sticky and brown to black in
colour. The fry hatch within 24—36 hours. The body of young fish is
translucent, but the yolk sac is dark. After about three days they already have black eyes. They swim easily after five to six days. During this
period they loose their shyness completely, swim freely about the glass
tank and do not hide in the plants. At first they prefer rotifers and the
Cyclops nauplii. They grow well.

28

Red or **Rummy-nosed Tetra** (28) is a native of the lower Amazon basin and grows to about
Hemigrammus　4 cm long. The imported fish, although shy at the beginning, soon get
rhodostomus　accustomed to life in captivity. The sexual differences are shown in
picture 28 (male below, female above). For many years, this species
was confused with the Red-headed Tetra. Literature on the reproduction of the Red Tetra should therefore be regarded with caution.

Red-headed Tetra (29) comes from the Río Huallaga on the upper reaches of the Amazon,
Petitella georgiae　and from the neighbourhood of Iquitos in Peru. The females are fairly big,
some reaching a length of 6 cm. The males are smaller and more slen-
der (see drawing). The black crescent-shaped mark at the base of the
tail is a conspicuous feature which distinguishes this fish from the Red
Tetra. The colour of the tail fin is also different in the two species. In
P. georgiae, the red colour of the head extends only as far as the gill
covers, whereas in the Red Tetra it continues to form a wedge on the
flanks, extending up to the dorsal fin (Fig. 28). For spawning in the
aquarium, *Petitella* needs soft water kept at about 25° C. The fish are
not very productive. The fry hatch within some 30—36 hours.

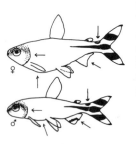

Petitella georgiae

46

30

Neon Tetra (30, 31, 32) lives in the upper reaches of the Amazon and Río Purus. It grows to
Paracheirodon innesi a length of 4 cm. The female is bigger than the male. For years the
Neon Tetra belonged among the 'problematic fishes'. Only after World
War II did aquarists discover the requirements for breeding. The water
must be very soft, 1—2° dNCH (without carbonate hardness), and the
pH should range between 6.2 and 6.8. A small admixture of peat extract
is essential. The spawning temperature should be kept between 23 and
24°C. The breeding pair spawn over plants and must be removed from
the tank immediately after spawning, otherwise they will eat the eggs.
The fry hatch after about 24 hours and learn to swim five days later.
One spawning yields 70—250 young. After 14 days the young take on
a red colour and the green-blue glittering stripe on their body appears at

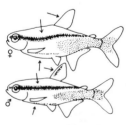

Paracheirodon innesi

48

the age of 18—21 days. Except for the spawning period, the breeding fish should be kept in colder water at temperatures lower than 20°C. At temperatures above 24°C the eggs quickly ripen in the females and spontaneously leave the body cavity without being fertilized. Females kept at above 24°C are not willing to spawn; their ventral line is straight, they resemble the males, seek fights, and are often unable to reproduce.

Cardinal Tetra (33)
Cheirodon axelrodi
lives in the southern tributaries of the Río Negro and the basin of the Orinoco. Fish imported from different localities differ in size and often in fin colouration. The females are bigger than the males and grow to a length of 5 cm. When their eggs are ripe, the female's belly is so

49

deformed that they look as if they are suffering from dropsy (see drawing). They spawn in open water at twilight and sometimes at night, or under weak artificial light. The eggs develop properly in soft water (about 1° dNCH) at a low pH value (5 to 5.5) without the addition of peat extract. At water temperature from 27 to 28°C the fry hatch within 18—20 hours. The young spend the next four days lying on the bottom and on the fifth or sixth day they fill their swimbladders and start swimming. They are very shy and sensitive to vibrations and abrupt changes of light. The Cardinal Tetra is highly fertile and 400 to 600 eggs from one female in one spawning are not exceptional. The fry grow very slowly. For five to six weeks they must be given live 'powder' food, rotifers, nauplii of *Cyclops* or brine shrimps, and should be fed a little several times a day. At the age of five weeks the fry are green coloured (longitudinal stripe) and their size is similar to that of the Neon Tetra when 17 days old.

Other South American representatives of *Cheirodon*, such as *C. piaba*, *C. meinkeni* and *C. leusciscus*, have occasionally been imported. Only some of these have been successfully reproduced in captivity.

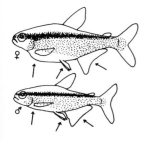

Cheirodon axelrodi

51

34

Black Tetra (34) comes from the territory of Mato Grosso on the Río Paraguay and the Río
Gymnocorymbus   Negro. It is a smaller characin, about 5.5 cm long, with flattened body
ternetzi   sides. The dorsal surface is not covered with scales, the adipose fin is
well-developed, and the dorsal and anal fins are comparatively large.
The lateral line runs along the full length of the body and the premaxil-
la is armed with two rows of teeth. It is easy to keep, even for a begin-
ner. It can survive temperatures as low as 16°C. Half-grown fishes are
a splendid velvet black. The intensity of the colour disappears with age,
particularly in females which eventually become light grey. The females are always larger than the males and can be distinguished by
a differently shaped swimbladder when looked at from the side against
light. Larger tanks must be used for spawning since the fish are shy and

reluctant to spawn in small aquariums. A short courtship display always precedes spawning; then the female is chased by the male and the pair spawn while vibrating their fins. Tapwater which has been left to stand for some time will suffice for the fish to spawn; the general hardness of such water should not be higher than 8° dGH. The fry hatch from translucent eggs within some 26—34 hours, and the eleutherembryos spend another five to six days attached to the walls of the tank. After this time they fill their swimbladders and start hunting for their own food. It is best to give the fry live food such as rotifers and *Cyclops* nauplii. The fry grow very quickly. It is impressive to watch a large shoal of the young which look as if they had no tails; this illusion is caused by their translucent caudal fin. They all follow the same course and change direction together as if they were joined together. The Black Tetra rarely suffers from disease. It causes few maintenance problems as it does not overeat and does not cause excessive pollution of its environment.

Silver Tetra (35) is an olive-grey to green characin from the coastal waters of the northern part
Ctenobrycon spilurus of South America. The adult fish grow up to 8 cm long. The females are slightly larger than the males; they are also paler and their belly is more markedly convex. The Silver Tetra is an omnivorous species and prospers in aquariums with ample aquatic vegetation. They withstand large fluctuations of temperature without difficulty, so that they can be kept in winter at varying room temperatures without heating the water. Breeding is easy. The pair swim quickly through the tank when spawning; the female deposits her eggs in a tangle of fine-leaved plants while the male continues his courtship display. The fry leave the egg case after 24 hours at 26° C. The progeny (several hundred young fish) grow fair quickly.

36

Blind Cave-fish (36) inhabits the underground waters of the limestone caves (Cueva Chica) in *Anoptichthys jordani* the province of San Luis Potosí, Mexico. It is closely related to the surface-water subspecies *Astyanax fasciatus mexicanus* with which it can be successfully crossed, with the production of fertile hybrids. This is why some ichthyologists do not treat it as a separate species, claiming that it is just a cave form of *A. f. mexicanus*. When kept under light in aquariums, the Blind Cave-fish changes its usual meat-red colour for silver. It grows to about 12 cm in length. The males are smaller than the females. The water should be hard (at least 15° dGH) and rather warm

37

38

(26—27°C) to match water conditions in its natural environment. Fry emerge from the eggs with clearly visible black eyes. However, the eyes are not used for seeing, do not grow and steadily reduce in size. At fifty-two days the eyes become completely enclosed in a cartilaginous sheath which has developed from the white of the eye and it is covered with a thick layer of fat.

Exodon paradoxus (37) lives in the waters of the Río Branco and Rupununi in the northern part of South America. With its colourful appearance it would be a popular aquarium species were it not for its highly predaceous habits. The eggs are laid on plants and the fry hatch within 25—30 hours at 26—28°C. The species is hard to breed and rear. It is only rarely imported.

Bloodfin (38) is a native of the Paraná in Argentina. Many other species of the genus *Aphyo-*
Aphyocharax anisitsi   *charax* are imported from time to time, but they have never become permanently acclimatized in aquariums. The Bloodfin is a lively and mod-

55

est little fish which prefers sunflooded aquariums. It grows to a length of about 5.5 cm. When spawning, it lays eggs on plants. The fry hatch at 24—28°C within about 30 hours. At first the young hang attached to the walls of the tank, to plants, or even to the water-surface membrane. After five days they will eat small live food as well as dry and artificial feed. The water in which the Bloodfin is kept must be crystalline-pure throughout its life.

Cochu's Blue Tetra (39) was captured in running waters near Loreto Yacu in the basin of the
Boehlkea fredcochui Amazon. Dr. J. Géry, a French ichthyologist, believes it also lives in the area of Marañón between the cities of Iquitos and Leticia. The body colour of this species, particularly pronounced in the male, is metallic blue to light blue. It grows to about 4 cm.

European aquarists may know this species under the synonym *Microbrycon cochui.* Nothing certain is known about rearing this fish in captivity.

Sharp-toothed Tetra (40) inhabits the fresh waters of Africa, from the estuary of the Nile to
Micralestes acutidens   Zambia and the Limpopo. It grows to a length of about 7 cm. It will
display its full colours only in weakly acidic water at a temperature of
25—27°C. Spawning, which requires soft water with non-carbonate
hardness up to 5° dNCH, looks violent and is rarely successful in captivity. Mere traces of carbonates kill the embryos in the egg cover. The
species exists in many colours and sizes, across its wide distribution.

Emperor Tetra (41) comes from the Río San Juan and other waters in Columbia. The male is
Nematobrycon   larger, about 7 cm long. The number of eggs ranges between 20 and
palmeri   100. The fry prosper only in soft water up to 5° dNCH at zero carbonate hardness and at a very low pH (between 5.5 and 6.0). Old rain or
snow water is best for this species. If water which was filtered through
peat is used the fry hatch with difficulty and most of them die. Thirty
hours later and at an optimum temperature between 24 and 26°C the
eleutherembryos abandon the egg cover. Five days after they started

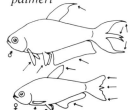

57

42

swimming the fry should be given live 'powder' food for the first time. Half-grown individuals can survive an incredibly low pH of 4. Only at pH 3.5 do the fish start having difficulties with breathing. If this happens some of the water must be changed immediately.

Red Phantom Tetra (42) lives in the Río Muco and in the upper part of the Río Meta in South *Megalamphodus* America. It is about 4 cm in length. The water in which the fish is to be *sweglesi* bred should be soft and slightly acid. The average number of young from one spawning ranges between 150 and 300. The fry grow very quickly. A shoal of orange-coloured fish in the green of an aquarium looks very conspicuous and attractive. The Red Phantom Tetra does not live long and often suffers from dropsy and plistophorosis. Another

43

44

popular aquarium species is its close relative, the Black Phantom Tetra *(Megalamphodus megalopterus)* from the Río Guaporé. It is fascinating to watch two males in threat display. The male has larger fins than the female and the colour of the fins is also different; the pelvic fins and the adipose fin are red in the female and grey to black in the male. The fry of the Black Phantom Tetra grow very slowly. Both species need water of the same temperature (from 23 to 26°C).

Diamond Tetra (43) comes from Venezuela and grows to about 6 cm long. It is not difficult to
Moenkhausia pittieri breed and rear this species, although it demands water of high quality, about the same as for the Neon Tetra *(Hyphessobrycon innesi)*. The adults need a lot of space, hence the tank must be large.

Swordtailed Characin (44) inhabits the waters of Trinidad and northern Venezuela. The males
Stevardia riisei grow up to 7 cm long and are larger than the females; their gill cover

59

45

protrudes into a spoon-shaped process with a 'mirror' at the end. This charmin is undemanding but prospers only in aquariums with sufficient vegetation. The courtship displays of this fish are interesting since the eggs are fertilized internally. The female then lays the eggs in the absence of the male. The fry hatch within 20—36 hours, the incubation time depending on water temperature (25—28°C).

46

Yellow Congo Characin (45) is a native of the lower course of the Congo River and grows to
Hemigrammopeter-   a length of about 8 cm. If not kept in a shoal it remains pale and dimly
sius caudalis   coloured in community aquariums. It prefers soft and slightly acid water. In captivity the female produces eggs with difficulty. As in the
majority of African characins, this is due to a shortage of suitable food,
particularly insects. The initial growth of the young is very slow. Breeding is generally similar to that of the Congo Tetra *(Phenacogrammus
interruptus).*

Penguin Fish (46) comes from the Río Guaporé, a tributary of the Amazon. It grows to a length
Thayeria obliqua   of 8 cm. The species *T. sanctaemariae,* which is described later, and
T. obliqua should be considered as the same species. The Penguin Fish
is a lively and decorative fish, but unfortunately aquarists are entirely
dependent on imports from its natural habitat since it has not yet reproduced in captivity. It is omnivorous but prefers plankton food. For
many years it has often been confused with the following species.

Thayeria boehlkei (47) is found in the upper courses of the Marañón, a tributary of the Amazon. It grows to the length of 6 cm. Its lateral dark band extends from
the hind edge of the gill cover. The body colour is the same in both
sexes. The female looks fuller in the pelvic region during the spawning

61

48

period. There is also a difference in the shape of the swimbladder. Adult fish can be kept only in a well-covered aquarium since they are good jumpers. When fished with a net, imported individuals may jump a distance of two metres. For breeding this species, larger spawning tanks must be used with 30—40 litres of soft water at 3—5° dNCH and zero carbonate hardness. The optimal breeding temperature is 26°C. Aquatic plants are not necessary for breeding. The fish spawn in the evening under dim light and the spawning looks violent. The pH of the water should be kept above 7.0 throughout the development of the embryos and after hatching. Only live 'powder' food should be given to the swimming fry. The young fish grow quickly. When four weeks old, the fish is 10—12 mm long. A thousand young from one spawning is not exceptional.

Rachow's Pyrrhulina or **Fanning Characin** (48) is a native of the lower reaches of the Paraná
Pyrrhulina and La Plata. It grows to 5—7 cm. The sexes differ only in the shape of
rachoviana the belly which is more convex in the female. It spawns readily on the
leaves of plants or in small pits in sand.

Neolebias trilineatus (49) inhabits the shallow coastal waters of the upper Congo. The female
is larger and grows to 4 cm long. This fish has been known in Europe
for some time under the commercial name 'Goldneon'. It spawns in soft
water in a thicket of plants. The fry are very shy. The fish have beautiful colours but their productivity is low.

Ansorge's Neolebias (50) is a native of central Africa. The adult females are larger than the
Neolebias ansorgei males and are only 3.5 cm long. The fish prefer densely overgrown

63

50

51

aquariums with numerous hiding places. Throughout life they need soft and slightly acid water. The breeding temperature of the water should be between 24 to 30°C. A spawning may produce up to three hundred small eggs which are deposited by the female in a thicket of fine-leaved plants. The fish reach sexual maturity at six to eight months. Care and breeding are difficult since young as well as adult fish are very sensitive to even a small amount of water being replaced during the cleaning of the tank. The names *N. landgrafi* and *N. geisleri* are synonyms of this species.

One-striped African Characin (51) comes from the fresh waters of equatorial Africa. The *Nannaethiops unitaeniatus* female, which grows to a length of 7 cm, is larger than the male. This characin has no special requirements for food and willingly eats any live food. It is very productive but not very popular among aquarists because it has rather sober colouring and is shy. For spawning it needs soft water at 25—27°C and a thicket of fine-leaved plants. At 25°C the young hatch from the eggs within 26 hours.

Red-spotted Copeina (52) is a characin which grows up to 15 cm long. It comes from the middle *Copeina guttata* reaches of the Amazon. In captivity it prospers in medium-hard water at a temperature of 22—28°C. Like Rachow's Pyrrhulina, the breeding pair lay eggs on the broad leaves of water plants, on flat stones, or most frequently, into a small pit which the fish dig out in the sand as a cradle for the young. Up to 500 eggs can be produced by one female. The female should be removed after spawning. The act of spawning lasts two to four hours. The fry hatch after about 36 hours and are sensitive to temperature fluctuations.

Dwarf Pencilfish (53) is only 4 cm long. It comes from the waters of Surinam and West Guyana. The Dwarf Pencilfish is a lively aquarium fish, but its productivity is low. Very small, three-litre glass aquariums will suffice for successful breeding of this fish. The water should be soft, up to 2° dNCH. The eggs are laid on plants and are sticky for a short time after being laid. Then they sink to the bottom. A yield of fifty to seventy young from one spawning can be regarded as a success. Soon after contact with the water the egg membrane swells up and creates a large translucent sphere around the egg. At 26°C the fry hatch within 30 hours. They are resistant to temperatures as low as 20°C. Young fry have a catholic diet and advanced fry can eat large pieces of food such as nauplii of *Cyclops* and brine shrimp.

Nannostomus marginatus

A

A — *Nannostomus trifasciatus;* beginning of spawning — the male luring the female

53

Three-banded Pencilfish (54, 55) is widely distributed in the basin of the middle reaches of the Amazon, in West Guyana and in the Río Negro. The females are larger than the males and grow to about 6 cm long. The spawning habits of the Three-banded Pencilfish are similar to those of the Dwarf Pencilfish. When preparing for spawning, the male makes typical swaying movements, bending the caudal peduncle downwards and letting it flex up again (see drawing A). He then approaches the female from the side and swims towards plants as if showing her the way. This play may last for varying lengths of time. Females with undeveloped eggs take on their nocturnal colours (Fig. 55 above) and try to escape from the male by hiding in thickets of plants. Females with ripe eggs are normally longitudinally striped (Fig. 55 bottom) and follow the male, letting him lead the way. The male immediately returns to such a female, stops with his neck above the top of her head (see drawing B) and leads her gently towards the spawning substrate. This stage of courtship behav-

Nannostomus trifasciatus

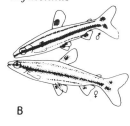

B

B — *Nannostomus trifasciatus;* just before spawning — the male guiding the female

67

iour very much resembles the courtship displays of the Tube-Mouthed Pencilfish *(Poecilobrycon eques)*. The Three-banded Pencilfish lays the eggs on both broad-leaved and fine-leaved plants. The optimal water hardness for the development of the embryos is between 3 and 7° dNCH, pH between 6.6 and 6.8 and temperatures between 27 and 28°C. The eggs are comparatively large and are about 1.5 mm in diameter. The embryos develop for 24 hours inside the egg case. The species is hard to breed and rear.

Espe's or **Barred Pencilfish** (56) was described as recently as 1956. It is a native of the Río Mazaruni in South America and grows to a length of just 3.5 cm. The sexes can be easily distinguished by the shape of the caudal fin which is long and spoon-shaped in the male. The spawning act lasts half a minute to a minute. Rearing in captivity is successful only in exceptional cases. The young grow extraordinarily slowly and are very sensitive even to the smallest changes of water.

Nannostomus espei

Nannocharax ansorgei (57) lives in the slow moving waters of Nigeria. It grows to 4—5 cm. The sexual differences are not known. In captivity it prospers in shaded tanks. It is the only representative of the genus *Nannocharax* which prefers plankton food. The other species of the genus feed on the fauna of the substrate (Tubificidae, Chironomidae).

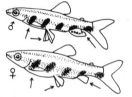

Nannostomus espei

55

Tail-eye Pencilfish (58) was first imported in 1949 from the Amazon basin and fresh waters of
Poecilobrycon Guyana. It is a magnificent and elegant characin which moves quietly
unifasciatus but often fights with individuals of the same species. It has been bred
ocellatus occasionally in captivity but no details are available on its breeding and
it has not yet become popular among aquarists.

Tube-mouthed Pencilfish (59, 60) also lives in the basin of the middle reaches of the Amazon
Poecilobrycon eques and in the Río Negro. In nature it keeps close to the banks near water
plants and decaying wood. It grows to about 6 cm long. In captivity it
prospers best when kept by itself. The fish will never show the full
beauty of their colours in the presence of other species. They always
swim at angle of about 45°. A ten-litre, all-glass tank will suffice for
spawning. The water should be soft, up to 6° dNCH, and the pH should
be about neutral (6.5—7.5). Breeding is often successful in old aquarium
water but water purity is the main requirement. The male is slimmer
than the female and its pelvic fins have white margins and white tips.
    Any broad-leaved plant will suffice for spawning. At each spawning
act the female ejects 1—2 eggs and sticks them carefully to the underside of leaves. One spawning may yield up to 200 young. The temperature of the water should range between 22 and 28°C. At a temperature
of 25°C the fry hatch within 24—36 hours and in 5—6 days start swim-

70

ming after one another. They need exclusively live food when very young. Sexual maturity is reached within eight to ten months. In aquariums the fish always keep in a shoal. The day colouring is shown in Fig. 59, the night colours in Fig. 60.

Naterer's Piranha (61, 63) is a piranha which is widespread in the Amazon basin, the Orinoco
Serrasalmus nattereri and the basin of the Paraná. It is about 30 cm long. Like the species *S. piraya* it belongs to the most voracious and most feared species of the genus *Serrasalmus*. Both species are kept in captivity only for exhibition purposes and in public aquariums. Breeding in aquariums is exceedingly difficult because shoals are gradually reduced, fish by fish. These fish are highly cannibalistic despite care and sufficient feeding, so that in the end, the strongest individual will remain in the tank alone. The piranha should be fed with fish, earthworms and, if possible, with lean pieces of beef, veal or poultry meat.

Despite all difficulties, some species of piranha have successfully reproduced in captivity. The fry feed well on the nauplii of the brine shrimp. About 16 species are known, six of which are kept in aquariums from time to time. The species generally look alike and correct species identification is usually very difficult.

61

Pike Characin (62) is an African equivalent of the South American piranhas. It is extraordinari-
Hepsetus odoe ly predaceous. The length of the adults is about 35 cm. Pike Characins
live in fresh waters from Senegal up to Zambia. In captivity it needs
large tanks with the water at 26—28° C, and must be copiously fed with
live fish and pieces of lean horse meat or beef. It is only suitable for
aquaristic exhibitions.

Marbled Hatchetfish (64) inhabits the forest brooks of the Amazon basin and various waters in
Carnegiella strigata　Guyana. It does not grow longer than 4.5 cm. In aquariums it is very
voracious and feeds on insects like all hatchetfish. It can be given small
insects of any species which may either be caught in the wild or artificially bred at home, such as fruit or vinegar flies, 'banana flies', small
cockroaches, crickets and larvae of gnats and chironomid midges.
These should be dried in advance and floated on the water surface.

Hatchetfish need space to swim about. They belong to that category
of fish which do not just glide but really fly. They move their pectoral
fins quickly, swim some distance near the surface and after breaking
water, fly up to 3—5 metres over the water which is a considerable ac-
complishment considering their small size. Their pectoral muscles are
strongly developed.

Common Hatchetfish (65) comes from the Peruvian part of the Amazon basin, from Guyana
Gasteropelecus　and Venezuela. It is larger than the Marbled Hatchetfish and grows as
sternicla　long as 6.5 cm. In contrast to the Marbled Hatchetfish, it has a well-
developed adipose fin.

The tank must be well covered with glass, but room must be left
between the covering glass and the water. In reflected light ripe eggs

75

66

can be seen in the body cavity of the females of some species. Some representatives of *Carnegiella* and *Gasteropelecus* have been successfully bred in captivity. However hatchetfish are not very popular among aquarists because of their special demands for food and pure water.

Banded or **Darter Characidium** (66) lives at the bottom of the rivers of South America from the Orinoco to La Plata. The female is more robust than the male and grows to a length of about 10 cm. The male has a row of small brown spots at the base of the dorsal fin. The fish has no special requirements for water composition and temperature (it easily survives temperature fluctuations between 18 and 28°C). The only recommendation is that the water in the aquarium should not be too old. This peaceful fish moves by jumping on the bottom. It 'stands' on the bottom, resting on its pectoral and pelvic fins. The front part of its body is lifted upwards while the rear part is supported by the anal fin and lower lobe of the tail fin (see drawing). Successful reproduction in captivity has been recorded several times. The breeding pair spawn among plants and the small eggs sink to the bottom. The fry hatch within 36 hours and start swimming after three to four days. They grow comparatively slowly.

Characidium fasciatum

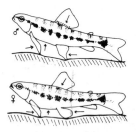

Characidium fasciatum

76

Chapter 2

TOOTHLESS BUT STILL MOSTLY CARNIVOROUS

Toothless jaws are characteristic of the representatives of the large suborder of carps, Cyprinoidei. However, cyprinoids have one, two or three rows of well developed pharyngeal teeth carried on the altered fifth gill arch. Their distribution is almost world-wide: they are found in Europe, Asia, Africa, and North America and exclusively inhabit fresh waters. There are large differences in body shape between the individual species. About 1,500 species of this suborder are known and many of them are used for human consumption. Those of aquaristic interest are mostly the colourful tropical and subtropical species of the families Cyprinidae (carps), Cobitidae (loaches and spiny loaches) and Gyrinocheilidae. These fish are mainly placid and undemanding. They feed on zooplankton or seek their animal food with their tactile barbels on the bottom. Some species are herbivorous.

Crucian Carp (67) lives in Europe and west Asia. Adults are about 45 cm long. The species
Carassius carassius exists in various sizes and shapes depending on its environment.

The narrow-bodied Crucian Carp from brook pools is designated as *C. c.* morpha *humilis.* The deep-bodied form from larger stagnant waters, lakes and ponds is recognized as *C. c.* morpha *vovki.* The dwarf forms, from pools and old river tributaries, are popular cold-water aquarium fish. In nature as well as in the tank, the Crucian Carp is very resistant to lack of oxygen. The adult dwarfs are only 10—15 cm long. Young individuals have a dark blotch at the base of the tail but this disappears with age. The dorsal and caudal fins are yellow-red in adults and reddish in the young. The female is more robust in spawning

67

68

time. The mouth is terminal and without barbels. The Crucian Carp lives mainly on plankton which is filtered from water through the gill rakers. The eggs (up to 300,000) are laid on water plants.

Veiltail (68) is a variety of the **Goldfish** *(Carassius auratus auratus)*. Over a period of a thou-*Carassius auratus* sand years, the Chinese have developed splendid varieties of Goldfish var. *bicaudatus* of many colours (grey, white, black, red and spotted) and many shapes (ovate without a dorsal fin and some with eyes projecting strongly along the optic axis which are known as 'telescope veiltails', 'comets' and 'lionheads'). They are bred with the greatest care, but nevertheless only a small number of first-class individuals are found, since most of

69

the progeny return to the initial wild form in both shape and colours. Veiltail breeding is a constant test of patience.

Pearl Danio (69, 70, 71, 72) comes from flowing waters of India and Sumatra. It grows to
Brachydanio
albolineatus
a length of 5.5 cm. The male is much slimmer than the female. Populations from different areas have different colours. The basic colours are green, shining gold, violet, and blue. Some of these colour variants have become common aquarium stocks. Breeding is simple. A small, 10-litre all-glass tank with tapwater which has been left to stand for a few hours will suffice for spawning. Shallow water, no deeper than 10 cm, is preferred by the spawning fish. Water temperature should be

79

70

71

24—28°C. The Pearl Danio likes to spawn just beneath the surface of the water, over a thicket of water plants (such as *Fontinalis* and *Myriophyllum*). Spawning is vigorous; its course is shown in pictures 70, 71 and 72. To ensure successful spawning two to three males per female should always be placed together in the breeding tank. If over-ripened eggs block the urino-genital pore the female then 'hardens' and is no longer capable of further spawning. The breeding fish should be removed after spawning to prevent them eating the eggs. The fry emerge from the eggs within three days (at a temperature of 26° C) and hang on to plants, on the sides of the tank or lie on the bottom. They start swimming after 5—6 days. Advanced fry keep near the water surface where they often shoal. Newly hatched fry must be given only the finest 'powder' food, preferably rotifers, or artificial food such as MikroMin floating on the surface. The growth of the young is rapid and irregular. The young must be sorted soon according to size to stop the larger ones from eating the smaller ones.

73

Zebra Danio (73) is a native of the eastern part of India and grows to the length of 4.5 cm.
Brachydanio rerio A temperature of about 24°C is sufficient for breeding this species in captivity. Some females are faithful to their mates and readily spawn repeatedly with the same partner. In winter the Zebra Danio can be kept in unheated aquariums at temperatures as low as 16°C. The requirements are similar to those of the Pearl Danio. The breeding pair usually spawns near the bottom of the tank.

Spotted Danio (74) comes from the rivers and ponds of Burma. It grows up to 4 cm long. Very
Brachydanio small all-glass tanks can be used for breeding in captivity. The Spotted
nigrofasciatus Danio is a warmth-loving species, spawning at 26—28°C at various water layers in thickets of fine-leaved plants. The breeding tanks

74

should be deep. About 60 eggs are produced by one female but two-thirds of these eggs usually remain unfertilized. It is therefore suggested that spawning fish be placed in the breeding tank in shoals. It is also advisable to shade the tank to prevent the adults from eating the eggs which settle on the bottom. Alternatively a fine-mesh plastic grid may be placed under the water plants to save the eggs which have fallen to the bottom. The productivity of the Spotted Danio is low. The fry are reared like those of the Pearl Danio.

Giant Danio (75, 76, 77) lives in the clear flowing waters on the west coast of India and in
Danio aequipinnatus Ceylon. In its natural habitat it grows to 15 cm long. In captivity specimens of only 6—7 cm in length are usually sexually mature. This lively fish spends most of its life near the water surface. The dominant individuals usually swim in the middle of the shoal. They have more pronounced colours and swim horizontally, whereas the weaker fish are paler and keep to the edges of the shoal, swimming in a somewhat

76

Danio aequipinnatus

slanted position. If the dominant individuals are removed their position is immediately taken by the next strongest fish. Rearing and breeding is similar to that of the Zebra Danio but because this species is larger the tanks should be bigger, with enough space for the fish to swim about. Spawning is vigorous. After each spawning act a cloud of eggs falls to the bottom. The fry are voracious from the very beginning and they feed on both live and artificial food. They can even be fed with substitute food such as a pap from hard-boiled egg yolk and a little water. They grow rapidly on sufficient food. Frequent cleaning of the tank and water replacement are recommended.

Fireglow or **Ember Barb** (78) comes from southeastern India and the islands of Sumatra and
Barbus fasciatus   Borneo. Adult males are 10—12 cm long. The basic colour is wine red
to violet with irregularly distributed black blotches which vary in shape
but merge to form five stripes. Three-week old fry have only three
transverse stripes. This species is difficult to breed. The fish are noto-
rious fighters and the male often kills the female. The eggs are very
sticky (a spawning plastic grid cannot be used) and the parents are
enthusiastic spawn-robbers. The requirements of this species for water
composition are high. The eggs and fry do well only in soft (2—3°
dNCH), and chemically and biologically clean water. Advanced fry

85

must be gradually acclimatized to harder water (this applies mainly to carbonate hardness). The adults, on the other hand, are tolerant of water composition and can live for many years in richly planted tanks.

Five-banded Barb (79) is a native of the Malay peninsula, Singapore, south-eastern Borneo and Sumatra. It grows to about 5 cm long. At breeding time the females of this undemanding aquarium pet are much larger than at other times. Their basic colour is yellow to orange and the fins of the males are dark red. One female lays 300—400 large eggs at a time. The robust fry hatch at a water temperature of 26°C within 26—30 hours and begin to swim freely and hunt for live food after six days. Rearing is easy because the fry grow quickly from the beginning. However the growth of the young is slowed down, or even arrested, at the age of 10—12 months. Commercial breeding of this fish is not profitable, since they do not command a high price and food consumption is high.

Barbus pentazona pentazona

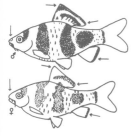

Barbus fasciatus

79

Barbus pentazona rhomboocellatus (80) has transverse bands arranged like *B. p. pentazona,* but the bands are wider and surround light spots. There is also a pronounced dark spot at the end of dorsal fin base. This differentiates both barbs from the remaining two subspecies *B. p. hexazona* and *B. p. kahajani* in which the spot is absent and the transverse bands are arranged differently. *B. p. rhomboocellatus* was introduced into Europe after 1975, although it was described by Koumans in 1940. There is no

80

information to suggest that this subspecies has been successfully reared in captivity but it is assumed that breeding and care are the same as in *B. p. pentazona.*

Tin-foil Barb (81) is a food fish in Sumatra, south-eastern Borneo and Thailand where it grows *Barbus* to a length of 35 cm. Large specimens make magnificent showpieces *schwanenfeldi* for public aquariums. The Tin-foil Barb does not show its splendid colours until it is at least half-grown. It is an undemanding fish, satisfied with water temperatures between 20 and 25°C. It greedily devours live food (*Tubifex, Daphnia, Cyclops,* larvae of gnats and chironomid midges), as well as dry food and lettuce. The fish also bite the soft stems of water plants. They grow rapidly with good feeding.

Barbus barilioides (82) comes from South Africa, Zambia and Katanga. The female, which is larger than the male, grows up to 6 cm long. This small fish has an elongate body. It is shy in aquariums and usually stays near the bottom or in the middle layers of the tank. However, if not disturbed, it is lively and likes to swim about. It is tolerant of the presence of other fish and can be kept in all-glass tanks of at least 10 litre capacity. It can be given food of all kinds. The water should be soft, about 3° dGH. *Myriophyllum* or *Fontinalis* provide a good spawning substrate. The temperature of the water should range between 24 and 26° C with a pH 7.0. One spawning may yield up to 250 eggs. The fry hatch at 25°C within 24 hours and start swimming freely after three days; they will take the nauplii of *Cyclops* from the beginning. After three weeks the young fish grow to 18—20 mm and have the first two thin transverse stripes on their sides. The sexes can be distinguished easily from the age of 4 months. The males remain smaller and very slender.

82

Spanner Barb (83) is a lively shoaling fish from the waters of the Malay peninsula, Singapore, *Barbus lateristriga* and the Greater and Lesser Sunda Islands. It grows to a length of 20 cm. The female is much larger than the slimmer male. The dorsal fin of the male is deep red at the base. Despite its comparatively large size, this barb is elegant and peaceful. Its productivity is high. The breeding tank should be planted with robust water vegetation since the fish spend most of their time near the bottom, always chewing at something and digging continuously in the upper layers of the soil. Finer plants would be damaged by them.

84

Island Barb, Checkered Barb or **Iridescent Barb** (84, 85, 86) is only about 5 cm long and comes
Barbus oligolepis from Sumatra. The males are larger than the females and are red to brick red at spawning time, sometimes with a violet or green sheen; the edges of their fins are black. The females are green-brown with irregularly distributed dark spots. The optimum water temperature is 21 to 25°C. The breeding pair need no special substrate for spawning, although they seem to prefer fine-leaved plants. During courtship the males are very active and can even be aggressive, but later their activity declines and at the end of spawning they are often quite tired. They must then be removed from the tank otherwise they and the females

eat the eggs. The small eggs are translucent and very sticky. The rearing of the young should not present any problems if live 'powder' food is used. Half-grown and adult fish are peaceful and sociable. Although they pick their food mainly from the bottom they do not dig in the substrate.

87

Sumatra Barb or **Tiger Barb** (87, 88, 89) is a native of the stagnant or slowly flowing freshwaters of Sumatra and south-eastern Borneo. It grows to about 7 cm long. The Sumatra Barb is a lively shoaling fish, which needs soft, well-filtered and crystalline-clean water. It cannot be kept with slow swimming fish because it likes to nip the ends of their fins. The optimum water temperature is between 20 and 26°C. Larger tanks should be used for breeding, since in large aquariums the male does not pursue the female so vigorously. Lower temperatures, between 21 and 23°C, may also contribute to less vigorous spawning. The water should be no harder than 3—5° dNCH and carbonate hardness should be lower than 1° dCH. It is advisable to add a small amount of peat extract. Six to seven hundred eggs are produced at a spawning. The eggs are large and yellowish, and the fry hatch at an average temperature of 24°C within 36 hours. After five days the fry swim freely. They are robust and readily take 'powder' food. They grow quickly.

Barbus tetrazona

Various mutants have been bred from the original form in recent years. The main ones are the yellow (xanthoric) forms with black eyes, albinos with red eyes (88), red-bellied albinos called 'Hong-Kong', and moss green lustrous specimens with transverse bands fused into a uniform background with a green sheen on top. These mutations are delicate and prefer warmth.

88

90

91

Longfin Barb (90, 91) inhabits the waters of south-east India, Travancore and Cauvery. It grows
Barbus arulius   to about 12 cm long. The female is more robust than the slim male. The male's dorsal fin has long rays which are dark to dark red in colour. Breeding and rearing is easy, although these comparatively large fishes are not very prolific. At breeding time a spawning rash arises on the male's body, with small white pimples mainly around the mouth. Species can differ from one another in the shape of the fins, in general colouration and in the elongation of the dorsal fin rays of the males. The breeding pair will readily spawn on almost any substrate: a tuft of fine-leaved plants, broad-leaved plants, flat stones or in open water in the corners of the tank.

Chinese Barb, Half-striped Barb or **Green Barb** (92) is a native of south-east China. The
Barbus   females are very robust and grow to a length of about 10 cm. This
semifasciolatus   barb is undemanding but needs a large tank for swimming about. It survives great temperature fluctuations (between 16 and 26°C) without difficulty, and is able to live in oxygen-poor water. It is best to have larger spawning tanks since room to swim about makes the spawning behaviour less tempestuous. The male approaches the female with an alluring dancing motion and drives her towards a clump of plants where the pair spawn. The yellowish eggs are quite small. The young hatch at 24°C within 24 hours. They are easy to rear and feed on live 'powder' food.

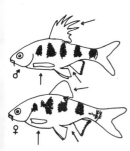

Barbus arulius

97

Golden Barb or **Schubert's Barb** (93) is a barb which is unknown in the wild. Its morphological *Barbus* 'schuberti' and anatomical characteristics are the same as in the Chinese Barb, so it is undoubtedly a xanthoric mutation of *Barbus semifasciolatus.* There are various intermediate types, such as spotted, pure gold, or even albinotic red-eyed specimens, and strange albinos with black fins.

This is a delightful aquarium species which attractively shows its glittering gold colour on a green background of water plants. It is also appreciated for its activity and restlessness. The Golden Barb is smaller than the Chinese Barb. The females are larger than the males, but their length does not exceed 7 cm. It is omnivorous and warmth-loving. The temperature of the water should not drop below 20°C.

Stoliczka's Barb (94) is a native of the lower part of the basin of the Irrawaddy River in Burma *Barbus stoliczkanus* and grows to a length of about 6 cm. It stands temperature changes between 18 and 25°C. The males are splendidly coloured. At water temperatures between 24 and 26°C the fry hatch within 24—30 hours. Rearing on live 'powder' food presents no problems. The adult fishes are docile and their colours are more pronounced in well planted and overgrown aquariums. They have few special requirements for water composition. The males often 'show off' the splendid colours of their dorsal fins.

93

95

Striped or **Zebra Barb** (95, 96) was imported from the Malay peninsula. The female, which is
Barbus lineatus larger than the male, grows up to a length of 12 cm in the wild and to
about 6 cm in aquariums. The body is elongate and the ground colour is
yellowish silver; the sides are decorated by four to six dark blue to
blue-black longitudinal bands. In females the colouring is less pronounced. This species is not very wide-spread among aquarists, although it is fairly prolific and breeds easily. It is a suitable fish for
community tanks, owing to its liveliness and tolerance to other species.
It is highly susceptible to infectious dropsy which may kill whole populations in excessively soft water or in old water with a high nitrite and
nitrate content.

96

Black-spot Barb (97, 98) comes from the western part of southern India where it grows to
Barbus filamentosus   a length of 15 cm. In captivity it is usually smaller (up to 10 cm long).
The males are smaller than the females and their dorsal fin rays are
elongated. Breeding is simple in large aquariums. The fish often spawn
in shoals. The young differ in colour from the adults; they have two
wide deep black transverse bands on their flanks, another narrowed
band at the base of the tail, and still another, fainter line, on the top of
the head. The fins of the young are orange to brick red. In half-grown
specimens the base of the tail is reddish with a red blotch in each lobe
protruding into a white tip.

Aquarists often confuse this barbel-less fish with another species,
Barbus mahecola, which has practically the same colours but differs
from *B. filamentosus* by having two maxillary barbels at the corners of
the mouth. The Black-spot Barb withstands water temperatures fluctu-
ating between 17 and 25°C.

'The Odessa Barb' (99) was introduced in Europe from the then Soviet Union in 1972, where it
Puntius sp. was probably bred for the first time. Its country of origin is unknown. It appeared on the fish market in Odessa in 1971. This fish has been subjected to detailed study and was found to be a relative of the Two-spot Barb *(Puntius ticto)*. It reproduces readily in captivity. The males display the splendid red colour comparatively late, at about 10—12

99

months of age. The eggs and embryos need soft water (up to 7° dGH) which is 25—26°C.

Black Ruby, Nigger Barb or **Purple-headed Barb** (100) comes from the shallow, slowly flowing waters of south Sri Lanka. The adults are about 6 cm long. It is suitable for beginners because it survives room temperatures of about 14—16°C in winter. Fish that have been kept at low temperatures in winter spawn very readily in spring at temperatures between 18 and 22°C and are very prolific. If kept permanently in heated tanks at temperatures from 20 to 28°C, they never show the full beauty of their colours and are reluctant to spawn. At spawning time the male takes on a splendid purple colour on the front part of his body and his head; his back is velvet black with a green sheen. This species likes to spawn in morning sunshine in a large, normally planted aquarium with sandy bottom soil. The composition of the water is not important. Adult specimens are omnivorous.

Barbus nigrofasciatus

101

Three-line Rasbora or **Scissors-tail** (101) inhabits the fresh waters of the Malay peninsula and
Rasbora trilineata the Greater Sunda Islands. In its natural habitat it grows to a length of
15 cm. In aquariums specimens as small as 6—7 cm become sexually
mature. The male is smaller and slimmer than the female. Large aquariums with fine-leaved plants are best for spawning. It is fairly difficult to
get the majority of breeding pairs to spawn. The eggs develop only in
soft water with neutral pH.

Slender Rasbora (103) is a native of the Ganges basin in India; it can also be found in Burma,
Rasbora daniconius Thailand and in the Greater Sunda Islands. Specimens of both sexes
are slender but at spawning time the female is fuller in the pelvic part.
The eggs and embryos need soft water for their development. Although a great number of eggs are laid, many become infected with
moulds for unknown reasons. The fry must be sorted by size at about
two months to prevent the stronger individuals from tormenting the
weaker ones.

Harlequin Fish or **Red Rasbora** (102, 104) is distributed throughout the Malay peninsula, Thai-
Rasbora land and eastern Sumatra. Adult specimens are no longer than 4.5 cm.
heteromorpha In Europe it belongs among the most popular shoaling fish kept in
community tanks. The male is slimmer and the lower anterior corner of
the dark wedge blotch extends up to the base of the pelvic fins (see

104

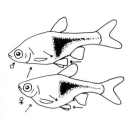

Rasbora heteromorpha

drawing). An all-glass aquarium with 10 litres of water will suffice for spawning. The optimum water hardness is 3—5° dNCH and 0—1° dCH. If general hardness exceeds 6° the mortality of embryos rapidly increases during development. The natural mortality rate from egg fertilization to free swimming is about 10 per cent. A small amount of peat extract is recommended. Water temperature should be between 26 and 28°C and the pH neutral. During spawning both the male and female turn upside down and the female attaches the eggs to the underside of the larger and stronger leaves of water plants such as *Cryptocoryne* and *Ludwigia.* The parents do not care for the eggs. After spawning, the parent fish should be removed. The fry hatch from the large eggs after 24—28 hours; they start swimming after five days and take live 'powder' food such as Rotifera and nauplii of *Cyclops* and brine shrimp. Their growth is rapid. The Harlequin Fish likes to spawn on sunny days. The main problems of breeding are associated with providing clean, soft water with the lowest possible carbonate hardness. A spawning produces 100—200 young.

Pearly Rasbora (105) comes from Ceylon. The adults are 4 cm in length. The male is larger than
Rasbora vaterifloris   the female and has stronger fins. The fish is splendidly coloured from pearly to rainbow. The breeding and rearing of the species is similar to that of the Harlequin Fish. The Pearly Rasbora prefers fine-leaved plants for spawning.

106

Bitterling (106) is a small representative of the carp family. It is widely distributed throughout
Rhodeus sericeus   Europe, (except in Scandinavia and Finland) and the coastal regions of
the Black and Caspian seas. It prefers the stagnant waters of the lower
courses of rivers, old and quiet river arms with a muddy bottom and
pools without predatory fish. At spawning time the females have a long
ovipositor (which projects from the urogenital papilla), for depositing
the eggs between the valves of the swan mussel *(Anodonta* sp.*)* or river
mussel *(Unio* sp.*)*. The eggs are fertilized within the mussel by milt
which it sucks in with the respiratory and feeding current. In return for
this service the mussel's larvae (Glochidia) are carried and fed by the
Bitterling until they fall to the bottom where they live independently in
the mud. The male Bitterlings are larger than the females and grow to
8—9 cm in length. They are conspicuously rainbow-coloured. At spawning time they have a spawning rash on the upper lip or around the

eyes. The Bitterling can be kept in aquariums where it provides a remarkable subject for public or private observation, particularly in cold-
water tanks.

Moss-minnow (107) inhabits stagnant muddy waters, which are densely overgrown with water
Phoxinus percnurus   plants in river basins flowing to the Arctic Ocean, from the Kolyma up
to the northern Dvina. The westernmost localities from which it has
been reported lie in the basins draining to the Baltic Sea, in the proximity of Cracow, Poznan and Gdansk. The main colours of this species
are brown to brown-green, bronze, or gold and it grows to 10—12 cm
in length. The Moss-minnow may be kept in cold-water aquariums. The
fish has no special requirements for water composition or oxygen content. It eats any live food of suitable size. It has not yet been bred in
captivity.

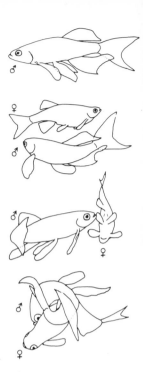

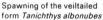

Spawning of the veiltailed
form *Tanichthys albonubes*

108

White Cloud Mountain Minnow (108) is an aquarium fish particularly popular with beginners.
Tanichthys
albonubes
It comes from the White Cloud Mountains near Canton and from waters near Hong Kong. It is about 4 cm long. Its colours vary greatly in the wild and in captivity. If it is gradually acclimatized, the White Cloud Mountain Minnow can survive winter temperatures as low as 5°C. Temperatures from 20 to 22°C are needed for spawning. The fish is omnivorous and lives in water of almost any composition. It spawns on plants in dense thickets of aquatic vegetation. The breeding pairs do not eat the eggs or the fry, so the young can be kept together with the parents. The fry hatch after 48—56 hours at 22—25° C and hang onto plants for three or four days; they then start swimming freely. At first they keep in a shoal just beneath the surface. They are best fed with dry and crushed food or the finest 'powder' food which they pick from

110

the surface. After 10 days the fish can be given nauplii of *Cyclops* and brine shrimp. Gold-backed or veiled mutant specimens (108) are also kept in aquariums.

Flying Fox (109) is native to Sumatra and south-eastern Borneo, but is a rare species. In the wild it grows to 14 cm in length; in captivity it is never longer than 10 cm. This species belongs to a special subfamily, the Garrinae, which have a sucking mouth. Most representatives of this subfamily have torpedo-shaped bodies. The edges of the jaws are sharp and are adapted for grazing on algae and other vegetation. Many species are easy to keep in aquariums at water temperatures between 22 and 26°C. The Flying Fox needs a large tank and has no special requirements for water condition and vegetation. It soon removes the covering of algae

Epalzeorhynchus kallopterus

111

110

from tank walls, cleans stones and plants within a short time and picks anything that is edible from the substrate. It will also eat animal foods of all kinds. When resting it lies on the bottom, on stones, roots or the broad leaves of plants. Although it prefers to live alone and drives all other fishes out of its territory, it does not harm them. In its countries of origin it is used as a food fish. Nothing is known about its breeding in captivity.

Siamese Flying Fox (110) comes from Thailand, from the upper basin of the Tadi river and
Epalzeorhynchus siamensis from the Malay peninsula. Adults grow to 14 cm long. Aquarists can only obtain imported specimens since nothing is known about either sexual differences or breeding in captivity. Care in aquariums is the same as that described for the Flying Fox.

Bala 'Shark' (111) lives in Thailand, south-eastern Borneo and Sumatra where it inhabits all
Balantiocheilus melanopterus kinds of ditches and flowing waters. In the wild it may grow to 35 cm long. As Meinken pointed out, the female has a markedly larger belly than the male, even when just 15 cm long. Only the smaller younger specimens are suitable for keeping in small aquariums. Adult specimens are good showpieces for public aquariums. The species is very hardy

112

111

and is omnivorous. It is a good swimmer and a strong jumper. It constantly searches for food on the bottom, looking under stones, or grubbing in the sand. Supplementary plant food is recommended from time to time, otherwise the fish may suffer nutritional defects. Nothing is known about its reproduction. Temperatures from 23 to 26°C seems to be optimal for this species. *Balantiocheilus melanopterus* sometimes produces short, sharp sounds. It prospers in the company of representatives of the genus *Labeo,* its close relative.

Red-tailed Black 'Shark' (112) lives in brooks of Thailand and grows to approximately 12 cm
Labeo bicolor long. Its ventral mouth is provided with two pairs of barbels. The lips unite to form a sucking organ, which is provided internally with sharp ridges and horny tubercles. The male is more slender than the female. This fish prospers best in soft water which has been filtered through a thin layer of peat. Frequent additions of fresh water are recommended. Water temperature should range between 24 and 27°C. The tank must be shaded and richly planted so that the fish has hiding places under roots, stones and so forth. Although the shark is omnivorous it likes to graze on coatings of algae and will also accept lettuce. Unfortunately, these fish often quarrel among themselves and should

113

therefore be kept in large tanks. The dominant individual defends a large territory which is often the whole tank and brutally drives away the weaker fish. Violent fights can be prevented by reducing the water temperature to 21°C but this temperature cannot be sustained by the weaker individuals. Spawning in captivity has been observed several times but never described in detail.

Bridle 'Shark' (113) comes from northern Thailand and grows to approximately 8 cm long. The
Labeo frenatus ground colour of the fish is grey-green to brown-green and the belly is bronze to white. The anal fin of the male allegedly has a black edge. These fish are very useful in aquariums where they eat any algal coating. They are much less quarrelsome than *L. bicolor,* but share some of its shyness and like to hide in flower pots or cut up coconut shells.

The genus *Morulius* is closely related to the genus *Labeo.* The Black 'Shark' *(Morulius chrysophekadion)* which has a strongly developed dorsal fin, is kept most frequently in aquariums. It comes from Thailand and the Greater Sunda Islands where it grows to 60 cm long. It grows quickly in captivity and is very voracious; it constantly seeks food on the bottom and is partial to any kind of food. The Black 'Shark' makes a lovely exhibit for large aquariums.

113

Chinese Algae-eater (114, 115) is a native of Thailand. The length of the adults is about 30 cm.

Gyrinocheilus aymonieri

It belongs to the family Gyrinocheilidae which is closely related to carps and carp-like fish. This family has only one genus; to date, three species have been described. They have no pharyngeal teeth. Apart from the usual gill-opening there is an additional aperture. The fish may remain attached to the ground for a long time without losing their respirating ability. They take the water in through a special aperture at the upper edge of the gill cover and discharge it under the lower edge (see drawing). The larger the fish, the finer their colours.

Gyrinocheilus aymonieri has a ventral mouth with well-developed lips which together form a sucker. The lips are provided with rasp-like folds for scraping the algae from the substrate. The fish is a stream-dweller and mainly inhabits brooks. In aquariums it is one of the best algae eaters, removing the algal cover from the leaves of plants and from tank equipment. It is not entirely dependent on algal food. Animal food, e.g. *Tubifex*-worms, dried and artificial food and dead plankton which has fallen to the bottom is also greedily eaten. The fish are very voracious. Larger specimens are often dangerous to other inhabitants of the tank. They can fasten on to other fish, damaging and injuring their skin. This habit can result in eventual death since the damaged

Gyrinocheilus aymonieri;
breathing while being sucked
by mouth to substrate

114

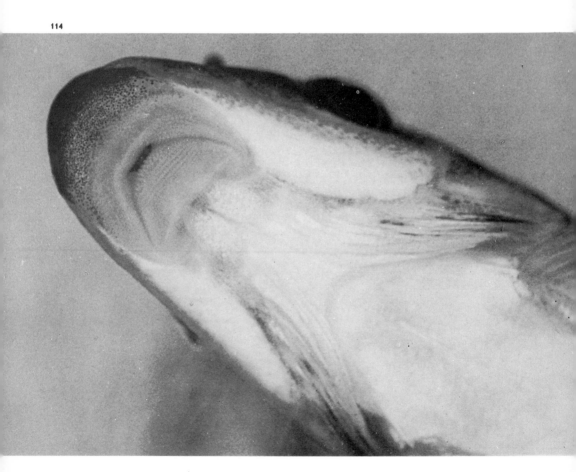

116

skin allows dangerous bacteria and fungi to penetrate the body. The young are normally very undemanding and peaceful but half-grown specimens and adults become quarrelsome and pugnacious. In spite of this, they are frequently imported. Nothing is known about their reproduction, either in the wild or in captivity.

Clown Loach or **Tiger Botia** (116) comes from Sumatra and south-eastern Borneo where it
Botia macracantha lives in flowing and stagnant waters. It grows to about 30 cm long but in captivity it is never longer than 15 cm. It has the most beautiful colours of any members of the family. The male is smaller and slimmer than the female and has deeper and more pronounced colours. The fins, in particular, are remarkably blood-red. Clown Loaches needs densely overgrown tanks, a soft sandy bottom-soil and crystal-clean water which is not too hard and is rich in oxygen.

Botia macracantha

117

116

Cross-banded Loach (117) comes from Thailand and does not grow beyond 5 cm long. It
Botia striata belongs to the family Cobitidae whose representatives are distributed throughout Eurasia, from Spain to the Pacific Ocean. Aquarists prefer the species of the genera *Acanthophthalmus* and *Botia*. Some representatives of the genus *Acanthophthalmus* have been bred in captivity, but species of the genus *Botia* have not. *Botia striata* needs a medium size tank with fine and completely washed sand on the bottom. The water must be well-aerated. This fish likes to hide, and live in shoals. If a small number of specimens is kept, they become shy and quarrelsome.

118

118

Botia sidthimunki (118) is a native of Thailand and grows to 4 cm long. These lively fish are very attractive when swimming in shoals throughout the tank. It was discovered in 1959 but is now exported in large numbers. The female is somewhat larger and more robust than the male. The substrate should be of fine sand with a small amount of detritus. The optimal water temperature is between 25 and 27°C. This fish devours any fine, live food.

Chapter 3   THE KNIGHTS OF THE WATER BEDS

Many catfish inhabit freshwater bottoms throughout the world. They are well-adapted to the benthic habitat. Their body is either naked or covered with a thick armour of bony plates and they are often decorated with bizzare spikes. Together they form the large suborder Siluroidei which includes some 30 families and about 2,000 species. The origin of these naked or armoured knights of the bottom is obscure. They have much in common with characins on the one hand but with carps on the other. Their mouth seldom has any teeth. This book will deal only with the most interesting species for aquarists, the tropical and subtropical representatives of the suborder. These are popular with aquarists throughout the world. The tropical and subtropical forms are mainly members of the family of mailed catfishes (Callichthyidae), thorny catfishes (Doradidae), Loricariidae, Pimelodidae, Pangasiidae, Clariidae, Ictaluridae, and others. Some of them have acclimatized in aquariums. Others, however, refuse to reproduce in captivity and must always be imported from their native environments.

Amblydoras hancocki (119) is a native of the Amazon basin in Peru, Bolivia and Guyana. It grows to a length of about 15 cm. The flanks are covered by transversal bony plates, each protruding to form a spine. The fish builds a nest from the plant leaves into which the eggs are deposited. When caught in a net it gives off quacking sounds. The fish seek hiding places at the bottom and feed on bottom fauna, such as the larvae of chironomid midges, tubificid worms and the larvae of various insects as well as on dry food that falls to the bottom.

119

120

Port Hoplo (120, 121) is found from Panama to Paraguay. It grows to about 18 cm long. The male is larger than the female and has larger pectoral fins with strongly developed, spiny armour. In aquariums it prefers a low light intensity. The male builds a bubble-nest, usually under a floating leaf. In aquariums yellow or white water lily, or even a small polystyrene plate, can be used as a nest-carrier. The female attaches about 800 eggs to the underside of the leaf (121). The male takes care of the eggs. At a water temperature of about 23—24°C the young hatch after approximately

Hoplosternum thoracatum

121

four days. If disturbed, the male sometimes eats the eggs or even the hatched fry. The male protects the nesting place and it is therefore advisable to carefully remove the female after spawning.

Aquarists often keep a close relative, the Armoured Catfish *(Callichthys callichthys)*, which comes from east Brazil to La Plata. In aquariums the two species have similar requirements but *Callichthys callichthys* is much less prolific. The number of eggs from one spawning is usually less than 120.

Upper-whiptailed Catfish (122, 123) lives in the Magdalena River in Colombia. In captivity it *Loricaria filamentosa* never grows to its natural length of 25 cm. Its body is very elongate and the uppermost ray of the caudal fin is strongly developed. The male is easily distinguished from the female because, besides other differences, the upper side of the male's pectoral fin is covered with dermal blotches which resemble dark 'hairs' (see drawing). The females deposit large orange-coloured eggs into various cavities under stones, and even into plastic tubes in aquariums. If the tube is cut lengthwise and the upper side is removed, the male can be seen sitting on the eggs (123). Free swimming fry are best fed with the nauplii of brine shrimp which move slowly in fresh water, and 'Micro' — eelworms of the genus *Anguilulla*. Later, at the age of three to four weeks, they eat 'Grindal' *(Enchytraeus buchholzi)*, chopped tubificid worms and enchytraeids. It is also important to give them ground up plant material, since fry fed only on animal food may die suddenly.

Aquarists often confuse *L. filamentosa* with its relatives *L. parva* and *L. lanceolata*. The different species can easily be distinguished. Adult *L. parva* and *L. lanceolata* have a thread-like ray on both the upper and

122

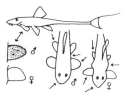

Loricaria filamentosa

lower margin of the caudal fin. Another species, *L. microlepidogaster,* which is rarely imported, has no extended rays on its caudal fin.

The representatives of Loricariidae usually inhabit the northern and central part of South America and live mainly in the flowing waters of small mountain meadow rivulets. The first fin ray of all the fins except the caudal is modified into a spine. The mouth is ventral and the lips are transformed into a sucking organ. As bottom-dwellers, they spend their life among stones and roots. The iris of the eye has a lobe which projects down to the pupil and regulates the amount of light entering the eye. This unusual organ has the same function as the iris muscles of all other vertebrates. Loricariids can easily be kept in aquariums in medium-hard water at a temperature of 21—25°C. Some of the species of the genera *Loricaria, Otocinclus* and *Ancistrus* have been bred in captivity. In general, all loricariids breed in the same way as *L. filamentosa.* All species prosper in shady places and spawn in crevices. Animal food (worms and zooplankton) as well as vegetable food (algae, lettuce leaves, spinach and the remains of various water plants) is essential for the development of these fish.

There are many genera and species of loricariids. So far, representatives of the following genera have been included in frequent imports: *Loricaria, Farlowella, Otocinclus, Plecostomus, Ancistrus* and *Stoneiella.*

Dwarf or **Rabaut's Corydoras** (124) is native to the small tributaries of the Amazon River near
Corydoras rabauti the junction with the Río Negro. It grows to a length of about 6 cm. Young fish change their colour twice before their colour stabilizes when they are about 3 cm long. However the full-grown specimens also differ according to the locality in which they were caught. It is therefore no wonder that this species is known under synonyms such as *C. myersi* and *C. zygatus.*

Schultze's Corydoras (125, 126) also occurs in many small tributaries of the Amazon. The adults
Corydoras schultzei   are about 6.5 cm long. They have an elongate body with a flat dorsal
profile. Figure 126 shows a female laying eggs in the company of two
males. Like the following species, the Peppered Corydoras, this hardy
fish is easy to breed and rear.

Peppered Corydoras (127, 128) is a native of south-east Brazil and the La Plata basin. It grows
to about 7 cm long and is one of the hardiest species. It is not sensitive
to water condition or temperature fluctuations. The best water for
keeping this species is medium-hard at temperatures of 18−26°C. The
addition of fresh water encourages spawning. Like other mailed catfishes (Callichthyidae), the Peppered Corydoras is also omnivorous. It

127

seeks its food on the water bed and prefers sandy substrates with layers of detritus. It feeds on tubificid worms, larvae of chironomid midges, half-dead daphnia, dry food and plant remains. The Peppered Corydoras was the first representative of the family Callichthyidae to be bred in captivity (in 1878).

127

All Callichthyidae like to associate in shoals; they live in slowly flowing and stagnant waters and have an accessory intestinal respiratory system. They are very useful in aquariums, since they remove all food residue from the ground. Most of the species survive temperature fluctuations between 15 and 30°C. Some species readily reproduce in captivity. During spawning the male uses the spine of his pectoral fins to catch the female by her barbels (127) and then turns her belly against his. The male discharges the sperm and the female lays three to five eggs into the 'purse' of her pelvic fins. Then the fish separate and the female swims through a cloud of sperm to seek a place for depositing the eggs. Sometimes she even cleans a place with her mouth before sticking the eggs onto a leaf, stone, or the tank wall (128). Some species produce just a few eggs, others several hundred. The fry hatch at 20—23°C after five to eight days.

Common or **Marbled Bullhead** (129) comes from the waters of the eastern United States. It is
Ictalurus nebulosus about 40 cm long and weighs about 2 kg. In the last century it was imported to Europe and became acclimatized in the basins of the Danube and Elbe. It belongs to a separate family Ictaluridae. Its body is naked and there is a well-developed adipose fin in front of the caudal

fin. In the wild it digs shallow pits in the water bed into which it spawns. The male takes care of the eggs and fry. The Marbled Bullhead feeds on bottom fauna such as tubificid worms and larvae of chironomid midges and on pieces of fish meat. Only young specimens are suitable for breeding in unheated aquariums.

Pimelodus ornatus (130) belongs to Pimelodidae, a family embracing many genera and species distributed from southern Mexico through Central and South America; it is absent only from the extreme south. All species of this family have three pairs of barbels, the maxillary pair being the longest. Many species of the genera *Pimelodus, Pimelodella, Pseudopimelodus, Rhamdia, Acentronichthys, Heptapterus, Sorubim* and *Microglanis* have been imported recently but breeding in captivity has not yet been successful.

Pangasius sutchi (131) is widespread in Thailand and is often imported into Europe. The optimum water temperature for keeping this fish in captivity is 22–28°C. It is very voracious and can detect live food at a long distance. If it is properly fed it will grow quickly. Nothing is known about the reproduction of this species. It has apparently never suffered from any disease in captivity. Frequent partial water replacement is beneficial for the health of the fish. The family Pangasiidae includes many representatives from southern Asian and Indonesian waters. The genus *Pangasius* has 15 species.

One of the smallest species, *P. sutchi,* is only about 20 cm long,

132

whereas the largest are giants among the family and exceed 3 m
(P. sanitwongsei). These giants seem to loose their teeth with age and
change from predators to vegetarians.

Angola Clarias (132) is widespread in tropical west and central Africa. This catfish belongs to
Clarias angolensis the separate family Clariidae, which is characterized by an accessory
breathing system consisting of paired tubular blind sacs extending
backwards from the gill cavity on either side of the vertebral column.
Clarias angolensis grows to a length of about 35 cm. It is very voracious. Small fish are frequently taken, particularly in the dark. During
the day the fish rests on the bottom. It has not yet been bred in captivity.

Chapter 4

FISHES FALLING FROM THE SKY

The tropics, subtropics and monsoon regions of south-east Asia and the adjacent islands, Africa and South America are inhabited by the egg-laying tooth-carps of the family Cyprinodontidae. They live in flowing and stagnant waters, and even in muddy pools. The adult males of all species are larger and more colourful than the inconspicuous females, which are mostly brownish in colour. The eggs are deposited onto plants or in the sandy and muddy substrate. Sometimes the fishes will modify the spawning substrate according to need. The eggs either develop continuously in permanent waters or, in ephemeral waters, their development may be interrupted by one or more diapauses. The species with interrupted development are called annual fishes. In the African species the interruption of development is usually shorter and lasts several weeks to months, whereas in the South American species the diapause may last up to two years. When the dry season comes the pools, which are entirely dependent on the supply of rain water, dry up and the adult fish die. Only the eggs survive in the dry and cracked mud until the next period of rain. The fish do not literally fall from the sky, but rain water helps to save the species in the most severe conditions. Most of the species are adapted to life in very soft water. As a rule the eggs are either sticky or their surface is covered with various filaments, hooks and threads by which they are attached to the substrate, and the egg cover is tough. About 430 species are known to ichthyologists and many of them are bred in aquariums.

Cape Lopez Lyretail or **Aphyosemion** (133, 134) inhabits muddy coastal waters from the Congo to the Gabon and grows to 5.3 cm long. It is a peaceful and placid fish and is content in a small and shallow aquarium. Very soft water, e.g. rain water, is the best medium for breeding this fish. The eggs are laid on fine-leaved plants such as *Myriophyllum, Fontinalis, Riccia* or *Ceratopteris.* Water temperature may fluctuate between 22 and 24°C. The fry hatch after 12—20 days and immediately begin to swim freely. They greedily take live food such as rotifer and brine shrimp nauplii. Their growth is quick. The aquarium must be covered with glass, since all species of the genus *Aphyosemion* are good jump-

Aphyosemion australe

133

134

ers. An orange mutant of this fish, bred in aquariums is known as *A.a. hjerreseni.*

Red-spotted Aphyosemion (135) lives in the waters of the middle Congo and in the basin of the
Aphyosemion lujae   river Kassai. It grows to about 5.5 cm long. The male's body colouring
is very variable. The conditions needed for breeding this fish are similar
to those required by the Cape Lopez Lyretail. The breeding pair
spawns on plants. The eggs, which are small (1.3 – 1.4 mm in diameter),
develop continuously. The fry are very sensitive and must be well but
carefully fed immediately after they learn to swim. Little success has
been achieved in breeding this fish in captivity.

Steel-blue Aphyosemion (136, 137, 138) is a widespread species which inhabits waters of virgin
Aphyosemion   forests and savanna in Nigeria and West Cameroon. The male is larger
gardneri   than the female; it is about 6 cm long and has large fins with a blue to
                     green sheen. The male's body is covered with 30 to 90 deep red
                     blotches which are arranged in irregular longitudinal rows. Owing to
                     the variation of body colour, correct determination has been difficult
                     for many years. In recent literature it has been referred to under the
                     incorrect names *A. calliurum calliurum, A. c. ahli* and *A. nigerianum*. In

137

the wild, a large difference in colour pattern exists between the two basic strains, one from Nigeria and the other from Cameroon. Breeding in aquariums is quite simple. The Steel-blue Aphyosemion spawns both on the substrate and on plants. The size of the eggs of some populations varies from 1.0 to 1.5 mm in diameter. The development of the eggs is continuous, with no diapause. At a temperature of 25° C the fry hatch after 12—20 days and immediately begin to swim freely. They

138

are very voracious and take any live 'powder' food of adequate size. The young grow rapidly. The sex distinctions are already pronounced at the age of two to three months and reproduction may be tried at this age. The Steel-blue Aphyosemion readily crosses with the Cape Lopez Lyretail *(A. australe)*. However the hybrids are not remarkable for their colour or body shape. They often suffer from various defects in fin shape, such as fusion of the dorsal fin with the caudal and anal fins.

139

Christy's Aphyosemion (139) comes from the middle Congo. It grows to 5 cm long. Two
Aphyosemion christyi populations or strains, with different chromosome numbers (9 and 15), are known to aquarists. If crossed by chance they produce inviable progenies. This may be the reason for the much discussed difficulty of breeding in captivity. The eggs are small, (some are only 1.2 mm in diameter), and their development is continuous.

Red-chinned Aphyosemion (140) is a native of southern Nigeria. It grows to about 5 cm long.
Aphyosemion In aquariums it reproduces easily and the eggs develop continuously. It
calliurum is able to cross both with *A. ahli* and *A. australe*. In aquarist literature it is often incorrectly referred to as *A. vexillifer*.

Plumed Lyretail, Plumed Aphyosemion (141, 142, 143) inhabits the periodic pools of south-
Aphyosemion west Nigeria. The adults are about 5.5 cm long. In nature it spawns
filamentosum exclusively in the bottom soil and its eggs develop with a diapause. If

140

142

143

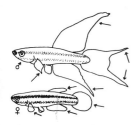

Aphyosemion filamentosum

the eggs are incubated without interruption in the aquarium, the fry hatch with difficulty. Better breeding results are achieved if the fish are encouraged to spawn in fibrous peat. Drained peat should be left moist for about 20 days, then flooded with water again. If kept in this substrate, the small eggs (1.3 mm in diameter) yield more fry of higher viability. Food which could rot should not be left in the peat together with the eggs, otherwise the eggs would be destroyed.

Red Lyretail or **Red Aphyosemion** (144) is very common in the Cameroons and Nigeria. It grows to about 5 cm long. The breeding pair spawns in soft, slightly acid water on a bunch of fine-leaved plants. The male is very active and often kills the female. One spawning which lasts up to several days, produces about 100—150 eggs. The breeding fish must be removed after spawning. The eggs develop continuously and the fry hatch after some 14 days at a water temperature of about 25°C. Spawning can be repeated after three weeks or so, as soon as the female's body cavity is full with eggs. The fish mature at an age of about six months.

Aphyosemion bivittatum

The Red Aphyosemion has a very variable body and fin shape and body colour, which may be bright brown, yellow, orange, green or blue. Owing to the variability of shape and size and depending on the place of origin, several species, such as *A. multicolor, loennbergi, pappenheimi, ringenbachi, splendopleure* and *unistrigatum* and subspecies such as *A. bivittatum holyi,* have been described in the past few decades. By studying the number of chromosomes and by crossing tests, Scheel has demonstrated that these are not true species but are only shape and colour deviations.

Aphyosemion bivittatum

145

146

Scheel's Aphyosemion (145) comes from southern Nigeria. The male is about 5.5 cm long. The *Aphyosemion scheeli* eggs develop continuously. Breeding is simple and is similar to that of the Steel-blue Aphyosemion. Most aquarists know this fish under the commercial name *A. 'burundi'* which has no nomenclatorial status.

Walker's Aphyosemion (146) inhabits the virgin forest waters of south-west Ghana and the *Aphyosemion walkeri* south-eastern part of the Ivory Coast. The adults are 6.5 cm long. This bottom-spawning fish is a typical annual species with a discontinuous development of eggs which are 1.4—1.5 mm in size. The development

147

of the eggs lasts several weeks. Adults often suffer from fish tuberculosis.

Blue Gularis (147) lives in pools in southern Nigeria and West Cameroon. Adults are about
Aphyosemion
sjoestedti
12 cm long. Most aquarists know it under the incorrect names *A. coeruleum* and *A. gulare coeruleum*. The eggs are 1.3–1.5 mm in diameter and their development is discontinuous. The female deposits the eggs in fine sand. If breeding is to be attempted, let the breeding pair spawn in a cylindrical container with sand on the bottom. Stir the sand with

Aphyosemion scheeli

143

a glass rod after a few days so that they collect in the centre of the container. The eggs can then be sucked up easily with a glass pipette. Place them in a Petri dish (of about 10 cm in diameter and about 12—15 mm deep) and cover with a glass lid. Leave the dishes containing the eggs on a table or in a cupboard at room temperature. Remove the non-fertilized, dead eggs every day to prevent infestation of the developing embryos. The incubation time ranges from three to nine weeks, depending on the temperature; after hatching they start swimming freely after two to five days and devour any live 'powder' food. A very small amount of trypaflavin can be added as a fungicide. The water in which the eggs are to develop should have no carbonate hardness, and its non-carbonate hardness should not exceed 5° dNCH. The growth of the young is very irregular. The fast growing specimens

148

must therefore be removed to stop them from eating their smaller siblings. The males usually grow faster than the females.

Playfair's Panchax (148, 149, 150) is a native of the Seychelles, Zanzibar and various places in *Pachypanchax playfairi* east Africa. It grows to about 10 cm long. The older males often look as if they are suffering from dropsy, since their dorsal scales clearly stand out in spawning time; this is due to hormone activity. The breeding pair stick the eggs to plants. At a temperature of 24—25°C the

144

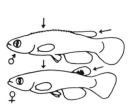

Pachypanchax playfairi

149

young hatch after 10—12 days, sometimes a little later. This beautiful fish is quarrelsome and offensive and it is therefore surprisjng that although many breeding pairs spawn almost incessantly they do not eat the eggs or the young. The parents can therefore be kept together with the young. The fry grow very slowly.

Géry's Roloffia (151) inhabits the fresh waters of forests and savannas in southern Guinea
Roloffia geryi   and in Sierra Leone. The adults are about 4.5 cm long. The male is

145

150

larger than tne female. In both sexes the throat is characteristically red, whereas in the closely related *Roloffia roloffi* the throat is dark. The eggs always develop continuously in aquariums. They are very small; only 0.8 mm in diameter. They develop quickly; at temperatures of 25—27°C the fry hatch after 10—12 days and within a further 24 hours they start to swim and take food. Water hardness for incubation should be about 15° dNCH with zero carbonate hardness.

Calabar Lyretail (152) comes from the coastal pools of west Liberia and grows to a length of *Roloffia liberiense* about 6 cm. It is a semi-annual species (it develops either with or without a diapause in the wild but always develops continuously in aquariums). It is easy to keep and breed in captivity. The breeding pair lay

151

152

the eggs on fine-leaved plants, in the substrate, or in corners of the tank. The water should be soft and the temperature should range between 24 and 26°C. Under these conditions the young hatch after 14 days. The breeding tank should be well covered since the fishes are very good jumpers and will even try to crawl out of the tank.

Sheljuzhko's Panchax (153) is a subspecies of *E. chaperi*. Both forms live in south-west Ghana
Epiplatys chaperi
sheljuzhkoi
and in the Ivory Coast. They grow to about 7 cm long. *E. ch. sheljuzh-koi* needs very soft water for breeding, and the pH of the water should be very low. Extremely low pH values (sometimes even 3.5) are known in the natural environment. However, such low pH values cannot be recommended to aquarists since, sooner or later, such acid waters become toxic to practically all other species kept in aquariums. The optimal pH is between six and seven. Breeding and rearing are the same as in *Epiplatys dageti monroviae*.

Fire-mouth Epiplatys or **Red-chinned Panchax** (154, 155) inhabits the fresh waters of south-
Epiplatys dageti
monroviae
west Liberia and it extends eastwards over the swamps up to the Ivory Coast. The adults are about 5 cm long. The male has an orange to orange-red blotch on the throat; in this it differs from the male of the nominal form, *E. dageti dageti,* which lacks a blotch.

Since it was first imported in 1908, the Fire-mouth Epiplatys has been incorrectly named *Epiplatys chaperi* in aquaristic literature. It is known as a hardy tooth-carp. Small, translucent eggs are deposited on

153

154

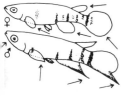

Epiplatys dageti monroviae

plants. At a temperature of 25°C, the fry hatch after eight to ten days. The fry immediately start to swim freely and to take small live food of all kinds. The general water hardness should not exceed 10° dGH.

Banded Epiplatys or **Striped Panchax** (156) comes from southern Guinea, Sierra Leone and Liberia. It grows to about 8 cm. It has a wide geographical distribution, and inhabits many different types of water. Because of this the Banded Epiplatys has a very variable body colour and shape. The coastal populations are less colourful than inland specimens and their bodies are more elongate. The Banded Epiplatys lives in the waters of virgin forests as well as in savanna brooks. There are probably a number of so-called sibling species which are hard to distinguish morphologically from one another with certainty. Tests to cross the different populations yield infertile progeny. The spawning tank must be large enough, with floating plants which give good shelter to the fish. The males are quarrelsome at spawning time. The eggs are about 1.5 mm in diameter. The fry hatch after 12—14 days at 22—24°C. At first, the young keep near the

Epiplatys fasciolatus

155

surface. Their growth is irregular, making it necessary to sort the fry by size. Throughout their life these fish need medium-soft water with an admixture of sea water or kitchen salt.

Six-barred Epiplatys (157) is native to the waters of virgin forests from east Ghana to south *Epiplatys* Gabon. The adult specimens are about 10 cm long. The Six-barred *sexfasciatus* Epiplatys is easy to breed, like the Banded Epiplatys, but the young are very sensitive to changes in the water. They are also susceptible to bacterial fin rot. This is a long-living species and attains its most splendid body colours in the second year of life.

Guenther's Nothobranch (158) occurs in central Africa. About 20 species of the genus *Notho-*
branchius are known today and most come from south and east Africa.
Their bodies are comparatively deep and the scales on their heads and
flanks are provided with fine denticles. The eggs are covered with
attachment processes. Most of the species are hard to breed in captivity. Medium-hard water at 20—24°C is recommended. In soft water the
fish suffer from tuberculosis, dropsy, and are attacked by ectoparasites
(mostly *Amyloodinium*). Their productivity is high. The adults are omnivorous. The eggs develop discontinuously, preferably in peat. The fry

Nothobranchius
guentheri

158

159

of some species hatch after four to eight weeks, in other species incubation may last for half a year or longer. The young grow surprisingly quickly. If given enough food the young fish reach sexual maturity at the age of three to four weeks. The exact determination of the species kept in captivity is difficult.

Beira Nothobranch (159, 160) is a close relative of *Nothobranchius guentheri*. The female's
Nothobranchius body is irregularly marked with black dots. The fish comes from main-
melanospilus land Tanzania and the adult specimens are about 7 cm long. Breeding requirements are similar to those for *Nothobranchius guentheri*. These fish are bottom-spawners; their eggs are about 1.5 mm in diameter and they incubate in peat for six to eight weeks.

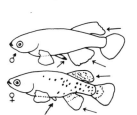

Nothobranchius melanospilus

153

160

161

Rachow's Nothobranch (161) belongs to a group of sibling species which lives around Lake Victoria in Kenya and on mainland Tanzania; it also extends southwards to Zambia, Rhodesia, Katanga, and Mozambique. The fish does not grow longer than 5 cm. It spawns in the substrate and the discontinuous development of the eggs lasts some four to six months. The tooth-carps of this group are very sensitive to changes in water composition and to other factors which have not yet been identified in detail. The outcome of breeding this species is therefore uncertain.

*Nothobranchius
taeniopygus*

Green Nothobranch (162, 163) was found as recently as 1972 on Mafia Island near the coast of east Africa. It lives mainly in permanent waters. The adult specimens are about 5 cm long. The fish is easy to breed. The eggs develop both continuously and discontinuously depending on environmental conditions. The breeding fish spawn readily in thickets of plants, in sand, detritus, peat, in the corners of the tank or even on an empty glass bottom. Most of the breeding fish do not eat the eggs. If the eggs are left in water they develop continuously at temperatures of 25—26° C and yield young after 18—21 days. If deposited in damp peat the eggs develop discontinuously for four to six weeks. The fry which hatch from discontinuously developing eggs are much more viable. Water hardness can range between 1 and 15° dGH without any harm to the adults, eggs, or embryos.

*Nothobranchius
korthausae*

155

Striped Aplocheilus (164, 165) is widespread in India and Ceylon. It grows to a length of about
Aplocheilus lineatus   12 cm. This tooth-carp can be kept in tanks only with larger fish since
the older individuals are very quarrelsome and voracious. They can
easily swallow a fish as large as a female of *Brachydanio rerio.* Breeding and rearing is very simple. The eggs are deposited on the fine-
leaved plants *Myriophyllum* or *Riccia.* The young hatch after 14—17
days in water of 24°C. With plenty of food of suitable size the young
grow quickly. The young fish are comparatively placid.

Species of the genus *Aplocheilus* are distributed from India and
Ceylon up to Thailand and the Indo-Malayan region. They mainly inhabit the forest waters. The females have a dark blotch at the base of
the dorsal fin and transverse bars on flanks. They tolerate a wide range
of water composition. Many species can be kept in hard water of alkaline reaction. Total hardness can be up to 20° dGH, but carbonate
hardness should not be higher than 7° dCH. If carbonate hardness of
the water is higher, many embryos die before hatching. All species
spawn on plants for several weeks in succession. The daily yield of
a fully mature pair is 10—20 eggs covered with a very hard and sticky
shell.

165

Blue Panchax (166) lives in the waters of the Indian subcontinent, Ceylon, and the Indo-Ma-
Aplocheilus panchax layan Archipelago. The adults grow up to 8 cm long. This tooth-carp is
panchax very quarrelsome, offensive and intolerant to fish of the same species
as well as to other species. Its eggs are large, 1.6—1.8 mm in diameter.
Colouration is variable and depends on the place of origin.

Selective breeding has produced varieties which have been incorrectly described as separate species, such as *A. lucescens* and *A. mattei*.
The subspecies *A. p. siamensis* has a fine red colour. It lives in Thailand
and aquarists know it as *A. rubropunctatus* which is not a scientifically
valid name.

Lamp-eyed Panchax (167) is distributed in virgin forest waters from southern Dahomey to the
Aplocheilichthys estuary of the river Niger. Its body length is up to 4 cm long. These fish
macrophthalmus like to assemble in schools and can be successfully bred in aquariums.

166

Aplocheilichthys
macrophthalmus

The breeding fish spawn for several days in succession. The eggs, about 1 mm in size, hatch in 10 to 14 days. The fry prefer very fine, live food such as rotifers. In aquariums the young always grow very slowly, however good the food may be; this is why the productivity of this species is so low.

Apocheilichthys macrophthalmus belongs to the separate subfamily of Procatopodinae which includes many genera and species that live in tropical and subtropical Africa. A few species are found in south Africa and Egypt. All these fish are good swimmers and move in a characteristic 'trembling' fashion. In their natural habitat they live in flowing waters of brooks and rivers. They are not easy to breed in aquariums since flowing water must be at least partially substituted by intensive

168

aeration. The fish stay permanently in the air stream bubbling through the water in the tank. They are sensitive to water composition and cannot live in excessively soft and acid water; even a low nitrite content is toxic to them. Hence the tanks must be perfectly clean and the water should be highly oxygenated. Some peat extract and an admixture of sea salt or kitchen salt is beneficial.

Green, Brown or **Cuban Rivulus** (168) inhabits the mountain rivulets of Cuba and Florida. It *Rivulus cylindraceus* grows to 5.5 cm. The females, unlike the males, have a very distinct dark blotch on the upper part of the caudal peduncle. The Green Rivulus is a good leaper and needs densely overgrown and well-covered tanks. It is quite tolerant to the presence of other fish. The eggs are laid on plants. The fry hatch after some 12—14 days and immediately start

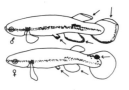

Rivulus cylindraceus

160

169

to swim freely. The young can be fed live food and are easily reared. The optimum water temperature is between 21 and 26°C. The Green Rivulus is very prolific, reproduces readily and is resistant in all respects. It is a suitable species for beginners.

Guyana Rivulus (169) comes from western Guyana and Surinam. It grows to about 10 cm long.
Rivulus holmiae   It needs a large, well-planted tank with medium-hard water. The fish is quite tolerant to other fish of the same size. A small and shallow tank with a thicket of fine plants will suffice for spawning. The female lays the eggs onto the plants. The eggs, up to 100 per spawning, are translucent and attached to a filament. The young hatch within 10—14 days and stay near the water surface after learning to swim. Rearing is simple.

170

Colombia Rivulus (170, 171) is a native of Colombia and the basin of the Río Magdalena. It
Rivulus milesi grows to a length of 6 cm. Breeding is similar to that of the two species described above. The large eggs are about 1.9 mm in diameter. Hoedeman doubts that *Rivulus milesi* is a good species; according to him it is most probably a hybrid between *R. elegans, R. cylindraceus* and, or *R. urophthalmus.*

The representatives of the genus *Rivulus* are distributed from the Yucatan, Florida and Cuba throughout Central America and the northern part of South America to the southern regions of Brazil. Taxonomic determination is often very difficult, owing to the adaptation of a large number of species to various environments and the very small interspecific differences. Perhaps Hoedeman's system of identification, which is based on the shape and number of scales on the front and top of head, is the clearest of all even though this system includes some intermediate forms of uncertain systematic status. Many of the 50 species of the genus *Rivulus* so far known are imported and kept in aquariums. All of them are good leapers and they are often seen stuck to the leaves of plants above the water surface or to the glass walls of the tank.

172

Ladiges' Gaucho (172) comes from northern Uruguay and grows to a length of about 4 cm. It
Cynopoecilus ladigesi lives in ephemeral waters. The fish deposit their eggs in the bottom-soil
and cover them with the substrate by jerking their body and fins at the
end of each spawning act. The eggs develop discontinuously. They
have a non-adhesive cover which is divided into hexagonal sections
with palmately branching peg-like processes. The male has the same
number of fin rays in the dorsal and anal fins as the female.

Cynolebias whitei (174) lives in Brazil in the neighbourhood of Rio de Janeiro. The male is
about 8 cm long when adult, the female only about 5.5 cm. During the
spawning act, the female tucks her head under the male's huge pectoral
fin. In this position the urogenital papillae of both fishes are closest to
each other. The eggs are laid on the water bed and are buried fairly
deep in the substrate where they develop discontinuously. The adult
fishes die soon after spawning since their native pools dry up during
a dry season. When rains flood the half-dried mud in the pool the fry
emerge from the eggs.

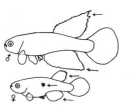

Cynolebias whitei

164

Black-finned Pearl Fish (173, 175) lives in the basins of La Plata and the Paraná and above
Cynolebias   Rosario de Santa Fé in Argentina. It does not grow longer than 4.5 cm.
nigripinnis   In its natural habitat it lays its eggs into fine loamy or clay mud which
never dries up. In aquariums the eggs can be kept alive for up to three
years in mud covered with a thin layer of water.

Many representatives of the genus *Cynolebias* live in the waters of
South America, from the northern regions of Argentina to the estuary

174

165

of the Amazon. The males have more rays in the dorsal and anal fins than the females; in this they differ from the members of the genus *Cynopoecilus*. About thirty species of *Cynolebias* are known so far. They lay their eggs in the substrate. Only seven species are popular among aquarists.

Peruvian Longfin (176) comes from the Loreto region of Peru on the upper reaches of the
Pterolebias peruensis Amazon. It grows to 9 cm long. Its mode of life resembles that of the species of *Cynolebias*. All the known species of the genus *Pterolebias* inhabit the savanna waters of Peru, Bolivia, Venezuela and Brazil. Their body is slim and the base of the dorsal fin is comparatively short.

176

The dorsal, anal and caudal fins of the male are elongated. All species are bottom-spawners. Dark fine sand or peat and plenty of floating plants are the best spawning substrates. Three to five species are occasionally kept in captivity.

Venezuela Killifish (177) is a native of Venezuela where it lives in the Orinoco basin. The adult specimens are 7.5 cm long. They are robust, intolerant, unsociable and require soft water and plenty of room to swim about. They readily spawn into the bottom-soil. The eggs (1.5 mm in diameter) develop discontinuously in five to six months. The breeding pair is very prolific and produces up to 500 eggs or more within a week.

Austrofundulus transilis

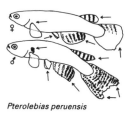

Pterolebias peruensis

Representatives of the genus *Austrofundulus* inhabit the savanna creeks of east Venezuela and Colombia. They are similar in appearance to the African fishes of the genus *Nothobranchius*. Only five species are known. *A. dolichopterus*, *A. transilis* and *A. myersi* have been kept by aquarists. *A. dolichopterus* is the smallest of them and only grows up to 5 cm long, whereas *A. myersi* reaches a length of 13 cm.

177

178

Cuban Killie (178) inhabits the fresh waters of western Cuba and grows to be about 8 cm long. It is easy to breed in captivity. The fish is thermophilous and prospers in warm water between 22 to 25°C. The spawning period usually lasts several weeks. The female carries a cluster of eggs for some time on a filament suspended from the urogenital pore. Later she transfers (sticks) them onto plants. The eggs are translucent and small. The young hatch after some 10—12 days; they are small and need the finest live food.

Cubanichthys cubensis

The Cuban Killie belongs to a subfamily, Cyprinodontinae, whose representatives are distributed along the eastern coast of the Americas, from Boston in the USA to Venezuela in South America and including Cuba, Haiti, Jamaica, and Curaçao. Representatives of the genus *Cyprinodon* live under extreme desert conditions in California, Nevada and Mexico.

Cubanichthys cubensis

168

Chapter 5

THE LIVE-BEARING FISHES

The West Indies, the southern United States, countries of Central and South America, down to northern Argentina, are inhabited by many live-bearing tooth-carps (family Poeciliidae). They live in various fresh and brackish waters. Sexual dimorphism is typical. The anal fin of the male is transformed into a copulatory organ known as the gonopodium. The largest species are no longer than 20 cm. The males are usually smaller than the females. Young are produced several times a year. The number of young per litter varies with the species and ranges from just a few to several hundred. The newly born young are fully developed and immediately capable of living independently. The female can bear several litters from one fertilization.

Live-bearers living in captivity need plenty of plant and animal food. The females of many species are cannibalistic and have to be separated from the young immediately. This can be done by keeping the pregnant female in a brood-cage from which the young fall through a narrow slit in the cage and so are out of the reach of the mother. Soon after delivery the young start hunting for live 'powder' food as well as dry and artificial food. Their growth is rapid. In genetic tests, or in breeding the best-coloured specimens, the young should be divided according to sex as soon as possible and the males and females should be reared apart. Most species tend to produce xanthoric and albino forms and these mutants are selected for aquarists.

'Wagtail Simpson Swordtail' (179) is a mutant of a splendid colour and shape and is artificially
Xiphophorus helleri   produced in aquariums. The ground colour can be green, red or white and characteristic traits are a beautifully developed dorsal fin in the male and smoke grey to black fins in both sexes.

179

180

'**Tuxedo Swordtail**' (180) is another cultivated strain with black body sides and a splendid
Xiphophorus helleri green-silver sheen. The ground colour is either grey-green, red or
white.

'**Lyre swordtail**' (181) is another achievement of aquarium culture; the males have a 'sword' on
Xiphophorus helleri both the upper and lower lobes of the caudal fin. The caudal fin of the
female has the same shape. A sword-like process is also found on the
dorsal fin and the pelvic fins are also long. Usually the gonopodium is
also excessively long and highly flexible. The males often fail to
copulate and the breeder must fertilize the female artificially to save
this splendid mutation. The ground colour of these fish is also green,
red or white.

A number of other interesting mutations (182) are kept besides the
three mentioned. All are derived from the wild swordtail *(Xiphophorus
helleri)* which has almost been forgotten by aquarists. Its native land is
south Mexico and Guatemala. The females grow to a length of 12 cm.
The males are smaller and the lower caudal fin rays are elongated to
produce a black-edged sword. The ground colour of the wild form is

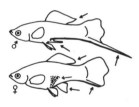

Xiphophorus helleri

grey-green with a reddish longitudinal band extending from the snout to the base of the tail. Breeding in captivity is simple.

Plenty of room and food should be provided for the fish throughout the year to allow them to grow to a sufficient size before reaching sexual maturity. In bad conditions they produce dwarf forms but this is not a genetic problem related to long-term inbreeding. Rather, the dwarfs develop as a result of a high concentration of nitrogen compounds in the confined space of the aquarium. It is therefore necessary to remove turbidity and add fresh water from time to time to save the

183

fish from gradual intoxication with nitrates or nitrites accumulating in the tank. It is also recommended that both sexes and different sizes be kept apart. There are up to 250 young in one brood.

Variegated Platy (183) comes from Mexico and its colour and shape vary as much as in the swordtail. The female is larger than the male and grows to about 7 cm. The males have no sword on their tail. The Latin name suggests that the species is variable and this variability is increased because it is easily crossed with most of the mutants of the genus *Xiphophorus*. Careful selection during rearing may result in the production of splendidly coloured males with fine and pretty body colour combinations — yellow, red, green, brown, grey and black, with differently developed

Xiphophorus variatus

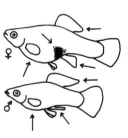

Xiphophorus variatus

172

fins. Black or brown blotches are usually scattered on the flanks, sometimes merging to produce bands. Three or four transverse bars extend
over the pectoral fins. A curious peculiarity of this species is that the
'pregnancy mark' on the hind part of the belly is also present in the
males, in which it is caused by the concentration of pigment cells. The
dorsal fin of the males is red at the base. Above the base it is mainly
yellow with brown blotches and bars, often with a black rim. The caudal fin is yellow or reddish while other fins are yellowish to grey-green.

'Simpson Platy' (184) has a strongly developed dorsal fin which may be either wavy like a veil,
Xiphophorus or firm and spread like a sail (particularly appreciated by aquarists).
variatus The ground colour varies.

185

'Meri-gold Platy' (185) is one of the most beautiful mutants of this species cultivated in captivi-
Xiphophorus
variatus
ty. The front part of the male's body is orange with lemon-yellow back and dorsal fin. The hind part of the body, including the tail fin, is blood red. These thermophilous fishes are hard to breed. The broods contain up to 50 per cent of non-fertilized eggs. A similar mutation, perhaps the loveliest of all, is called the 'Parrot Platy'. The males are rainbow-coloured with a metallic sheen.

'Red Platy' (186) is a cultivated strain of a bright red colour. The males are blood red and
Xiphophorus
maculatus
appreciated for the porcelain white borders of their fins. This, like further colour mutations of the wild platy *(Xiphophorus maculatus)* have low genetic stability. *Xiphophorus maculatus* comes from Mexico and Guatemala. The female is larger than the male and grows to 6 cm in length. Its original colour is brown to olive, with a blue sheen and with two black oval blotches on the caudal peduncle close to the base of the tail fin. A blotch also lies on both flanks behind the gill covers. Various colour and shape mutations have been developed in aqua-

186

187

riums. These artificially cultivated forms, unlike the wild fish, are specially sensitive to water temperature. Platies are tolerant to varying water composition but the pH should be slightly alkaline. They are not choosy and can be fed any live or dry foods, plant fragments, algae and so on. The brood, usually up to 100 young, is generally delivered in the early hours of the morning. The young are easy to rear and can be fed dry or artificial food. The optimal temperatures for breeding this fish are between 20 and 26°C.

'Comet Platy' (187) is a
Xiphophorus
maculatus
popular colour mutation with a red or yellow ground colour. The body of both sexes is covered with the same characteristic design: two black stripes, one lining the upper and the other the lower edge of the caudal fin. Neither the wild platy nor the cultivated strains have a sword; in this they differ from the swordtails. The different colour mutations must be kept separately in aquariums, otherwise long-term selection work would be spoilt by crossing. Crossing between mutants does occur in aquarists' shops where several strains are kept together in the

175

188

same tank. They give a magnificent colour effect but usually can no longer be used for breeding since the progeny, although many-coloured and interesting in appearance, do not resemble any of the parents.

'Moon Platy' (188) is similar to the 'Comet Platy' but has a large, round, dark blotch at the
Xiphophorus   caudal peduncle. Its most frequent ground colours are red or yellow. In
maculatus   yellow populations the males can have an orange back or at least an

176

orange or reddish dorsal fin. Very occasionally females show a similar colouration. Both mutations, the 'Moon Platy' and 'Comet Platy', are more or less genetically stable, comparatively resistant and easy to breed.

'Wagtail Platy' (189) is a mutation with a somewhat elongated body which is usually coloured
Xiphophorus   red or yellow. All fins are smoke grey to velvet black. The fish of this
maculatus   strain are particular about water temperature and are susceptible to various external parasites; in addition they often suffer from bacterial fin rot. The water in the tank must be pure and well-filtered, like that of the 'Red Platy'.

189

177

190

'Tuxedo Platy' (190) is a robust and deep-bodied strain, usually with a yellow or red ground
Xiphophorus colour which is only visible on the belly and fins. The flanks are black
maculatus with a splendid metallic green lustre. Individuals of this strain are resistant and genetically stable if they come from high-quality stocks.

'Calico Platy' (191) is a very variable strain of various ground colours from yellow through
Xiphophorus greenish, brownish and orange to red; it is irregularly sprinkled with
maculatus numerous darker spots of varying size and shape. The fish of this mutation are smaller and slimmer than other platies.

In general, platies are undemanding and can be recommended to
beginners. At the same time, they provide valuable genetic material
and are appreciated by advanced aquarists who use them in intensive
genetic experiments for obtaining new forms or for keeping the exist-
ing strains stable and improving their show qualities. Great patience is

needed for such work, which can last many years and even then does not always lead to success. Much credit is due to the American geneticist, M. Gordon, who has studied the genetics of platies for many years and has produced several strains. The 'Wagtail Platy', for instance, is a successful product of his laboratory. Apart from the platies already described there are monotone strains of yellow, blue, or even black.

Blue or **Spotted Gambusia** (192) is a common fish of Cuba, where it lives in waters lit with
Gambusia puncticulata sunshine and overgrown with water plants. The male is about 5 cm long. The female is larger, growing up to 9 cm long. It is undemanding and hardy, tolerating fluctuations of temperature and can endure temperatures of up to 30°C. It is also able to survive oxygen starvation. Live food is preferred. Breeding and rearing is easy and the brood number can be up to 60. The parents often eat their young. Growth is

192

rapid and sexual maturity may be reached within three to four months. Neither this species nor the other representatives of the genus *Gambusia* are very suitable for community tanks since they are pugnacious and liable to nibble the fins of other fishes.

Jacobs claims that all fish which are usually called *G. punctata* are, in fact, *G. puncticulata*. There is no information available about *G. punctata* ever having been kept in captivity.

Black-bellied Limia or **Blue Limia** (193) comes from Jamaica. The male is about 3 cm long
Poecilia melanogaster while the female is longer, growing up to 6 cm. The fish prosper best if kept singly in a well planted aquarium. They are rather sensitive to abrupt changes of water and to the freshness of water. Water temperature in the tank should not drop below 22°C. The males are lively and constantly harass the females. The brood numbers 60 to 80 and the young reach sexual maturity at the age of about four months. Besides animal food they also need plant food, mainly algae.

Hump-backed or **Black-barred Limia** (194) comes from the island of Haiti. The female grows
Poecilia nigrofasciata to a length of 6 cm and the male up to 4.5 cm. Breeding and rearing are the same as in the preceding species; the only difference being that the Black-barred Limia is particularly sensitive to changes of water. Before placing the fish into another aquarium it is recommended that the water be mixed for several days prior to the transfer. The fishes are omnivorous and thermophilous (22—25°C). Pregnancy lasts about six weeks and the brood number is low, about 30 young. The large young are 10—12 mm long.

180

193

194

Guppy (195, 196) is a native of Venezuela, the islands of Barbados and Trinidad, northern
Poecilia reticulata Brazil and Guayana. The female grows to a length of 6 cm, the male
only to 3 cm. It was brought to Europe in 1908. The fish has be-
come a highly appreciated object for genetic observations and experiments because of the great colour and shape variability, particularly
in the males. Aquarists have developed many cultivated strains and
these have provided magnificent showpieces for aquaristic exhibitions.
The show specimens are evaluated according to international stan-
dards. One of the most variable traits is the shape of the male's dorsal
and caudal fins of which 11 basic types are known. Females with splendidly coloured and strongly developed fins (196) have recently been
developed. At water temperature between 22 and 25°C pregnancy lasts
about 30 days. The pregnant females have a dark 'pregnancy mark' on
the back part of the belly. One fertilization by the male will suffice for
two to three broods or more. The males are typically polygamous and
very active. The young are delivered within two hours, depending on
the water temperature, its chèmical composition and freshness, and on
the environment, particularly the fish community. Wanting to protect
the young, the female may delay parturition by up to several hours, or
at least retard it. One brood contains up to 250 young.

Girardinus (197) comes from the fresh waters of Cuba. The female grows to 8 cm long, the male only to 5 cm. The fish is not very colourful and is therefore a little neglected by aquarists. The male's gonopodium is very long with two curved appendages at the end. In aquariums the Girardinus is peaceful and undemanding and lives for a long time. This species requires supplementary plant food (algae, lettuce, soaked oat-flakes). The number of young is about 60 and they must be protected from the female by keeping the mother in a brood-cage.

Girardinus metallicus

197

198

Dwarf Top Minnow or **Mosquito Fish** (198) lives in the waters of North Carolina and Florida
Heterandria formosa and is one of the smallest fish kept in aquariums. The female grows to
a length of 3.5 cm, the male only to 2 cm. This fish may be kept in water
which temporarily drops down to 15°C and the aquarium can be very
small (with three to five litres of water). The Dwarf Top Minnow is
omnivorous and content with good quality dry or artificial food. Unlike
other live-bearers, the female Dwarf Top Minnow does not harass the
young. The brood is delivered within six to ten days with some two to
three young delivered daily. Pregnancy lasts four to five weeks depending on water temperature.

185

Sail-fin Molly (199) is distributed in the coastal regions and river estuaries in the Yucatan. In
Poecilia velifera   aquariums it grows to 12 cm; in its natural habitat about 15 cm. The
males have a remarkably prominent dorsal fin. Many mutations of
beautiful shapes and colours have been bred in captivity. This species
has also been crossed with the species *P. latipinna* and *P. sphenops*. The
best-known of these mutations and crossbreeds are the 'Black Mollienesia', 'Lyre Mollienesia' and 'Veil Mollienesia'. Breeding and rearing in
captivity is difficult, owing to genetic instability and rigid requirements
for good living conditions and food (plenty of plant food and a temperature of about 28°C).

Pike Top Minnow (200) inhabits the waters of the eastern part of Central America. It is the
Belonesox belizanus   largest live-bearer of the family Poecilidae. The female grows to
a length of about 20 cm, whereas the male is only half the size. It is
a predator and is unsuitable for community tanks. Before copulation,
the male turns his gonopodium forwards and strangely twists and bows
his body. Feeding is not simple. Adult fish need large pieces of live
food such as small fish, dragonfly larvae, tadpoles, and worms of all
kinds. Specimens of 10—20 cm length can swallow full-grown female
platies or guppies without difficulty. Their upper jaw is movable and this
allows the fish to swallow large pieces of food. Water temperature
should be kept between 25 and 30°C. A point of interest is their ability
to change colour. The fishes are dark at night and lighter during the
day. The brood contains up to 100 young, 2.5—3 cm long, which immediately start feeding on small daphnia and enchytraeids. The mothers
often greedily devour their own young or at least harass them brutally.

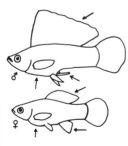

Poecilia velifera

187

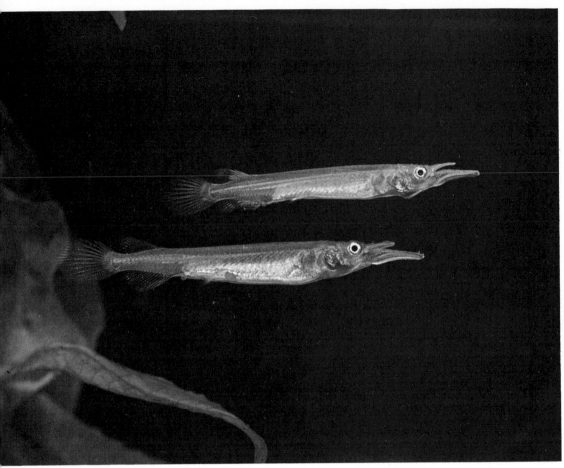

201

Sumatra Halfbeak (201) is a native of Singapore, Sumatra and south-eastern Borneo. The adult
Dermogenys female, which is larger than the male, grows to about 6 cm long. It lives
sumatranus in brackish and fresh waters. This species belongs to the family Hemir-
hamphidae. The females are fertilized internally. The sperm is not ejected via a gonopodium but through a transformed lobe-shaped anal fin
of the male. The fish feed mainly on insects picked from the water
surface. The young are up to 1 cm long.

Chapter 6   MONOGAMISTS WITH REFINED SENSE OF FAMILY LIFE

Perch-like fishes (Perciformes) represent a large group of bony fishes living in both seas and freshwater. The fish of this order usually have two dorsal fins; the first consists entirely of hard spiny rays whereas the rays of the other are soft and branched. The pelvic fins lie below the pectorals. The scales are mostly ctenoid. This order includes many suborders and families. Three of these families which show a well developed sense of care for the young are of interest here. These are the cichlids (Cichlidae), the nandus-fishes (Nandidae) and the sunfish and basses (Centrarchidae). Together, these three families are distributed in North, Central and South America and in Africa and south-east Asia. They lay their eggs on plant leaves (the phytophilous species), into small pits in sand (psammophilous species), on flat stones (lithophilous species), or into crevices. The young are cared for by the male or female, or alternately by both. Mouth-brooders show a very special kind of care; the lower part of the male's or female's mouth acts as an incubator for the eggs and a hiding place for the young in the first few days of their life.

Cichlasoma spilurum (202, 203) comes from Guatemala. The male (203) is larger than the female and grows to a length of about 10 cm. This species spawns in caves, a habit which, as some authors believe, is exceptional among species of the genus *Cichlasoma*. However, another species of *Cichlasoma*, the Zebra Cichlid, also prefers caves as spawning places. The fry of *Cichlasoma spilurum* hatch at 25—26° C after three days and the female carries them in her mouth into a pit in sand. After another three days the fry start to swim freely and eat live 'powder' food. Their growth is rapid. The adults are peaceful and look stately. They cause no damage to plants in the aquarium. Outside the spawning season they do not dig the bottom-sand at all.

202

203

Zebra or **Convict Cichlid** (204, 205) also comes from Guatemala, from the Atitlan and Amati-
Cichlasoma   tlan lakes. It is smaller than *Cichlasoma spilurum;* the males, which are
nigrofasciatum   larger than the females, grow to be about 8 cm long. The male has
markedly elongated dorsal and anal fins. The hind part of the female's
belly has a shining bronze colour throughout its life. A xanthoric form
with black eyes has been developed in aquariums. In a shaded tank this
milk coloured mutation is particularly conspicuous among green plants.
A female with the bronze coloured belly is shown in picture 204.

The original wild form of the Zebra Cichlid is brightly coloured. It is
very aggressive both to other species and individuals of its own kind. In
aquariums it keeps grubbing up and re-building the tank bed and often
destroys plants in the process. It will also nibble and bite them. They

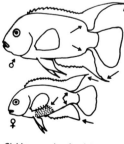

Cichlasoma nigrofasciatum

can be fed lettuce, soaked oat flakes, algae and the like. Meat must be provided as the basic food. The breeding pair will spawn in a pile of stones or in an old flower-pot. Sometimes a flat stone may suffice. The Zebra Cichlid has an unusual behavioural pattern designed to protect the young. When the fry hatch, the parents immediately transfer them to a small pit excavated in the sand or among stones. The parents change the hiding place if the environment is disturbed. The actual transfer of the young is both sophisticated and complicated. One of the parents tries to attract attention by engaging in very conspicuous activity, such as digging a pit in the sand in an open place. While this decoy activity is going on the other parent carries the fry to another safe place. The parents are brave when defending their young or eggs

191

against intruders which have come close to the hiding place. In picture 205 a Zebra Cichlid attacks the aquarist's finger without fear. The other breeding and rearing conditions are the same as in the previous species.

Hybrid between **Cichlasoma nigrofasciatum** and **C. spilurum** (206, 207) has been known for several years and the offspring are fertile. The hybrid displays an intermediate colour and can be clearly discerned from both parent species. Crosses between *C. spilurum* and the xanthoric form of *C. nigrofasciatum* result in weak progeny which never reach maturity. The breeding pair spawn and the embryos develop normally until the free swimming stage, but the young are never able to fill the swimbladder. Sometimes the young suffer from constitutional dropsy which soon kills them. Sometimes they will keep moving sluggishly, jumping on the bottom and even accepting food, but eventually they die. In crosses of this type two females often spawn together (206), one behaving like a male on one day and changing roles the next. Such pairs of females produce

205

206

many eggs but naturally nothing can hatch from the non-fertilized eggs and they soon decay. The females often fight with each other, each characteristically holding the other's mouth (207).

Barred or **Flag Cichlid** or **Festivum** (208) inhabits the waters of western Guyana and the
Cichlasoma festivum Amazon basin. The male, larger than the female, grows to 15 cm long.
Sex distinctions are almost absent; the male can be distinguished only
in the breeding season by the shape of the genital papilla which is
conical and pointed, whereas in the female it is cylindrical and is uniform in diameter throughout its length.

According to data in aquaristic literature this fish is peaceful, shy,
and does not destroy the water plants. However, this is not true at
spawning time, when the fish quickly devastate anything they can,
leaving only the remains of plants. When preparing the spawning place
in the aquarium, the breeding pair removes large stones and pieces of
wood. The sandy substrate is gradually transformed into numerous
heaps and pits reaching down to the glass bottom. These vigorous
preparations are usually followed by quiet spawning on a flat stone or
flower pot. Both parents look after their young with great care from

207

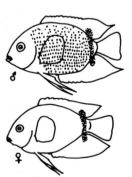

the very beginning. Having learned to swim, the young can be fed the
finest 'powder' food such as rotifers. If given coarser food (for example,
nauplii of *Cyclops*) 90 per cent of them die within two to three days.
The young and adults are warmth-loving and require temperatures between 25 and 28° C.

Cichlasoma severum

194

209

Banded Cichlid (209) is a native of the northern part of the Amazon basin and of Guyana. It
Cichlasoma severum grows to a length of about 20 cm. The male can easily be distinguished
from the female because it is mottled with red-brown dots all over the
body (drawing p. 194). The female is lighter and has shorter dorsal and
anal fins. Breeding and rearing habits are the same as in the Barred
Cichlid. Up to 1,000 eggs are produced per spawning.

Eight-banded Cichlid (210) is native to the drainage basins of the Amazon and Río Negro. The
Cichlasoma adults grow up to 18 cm long. The body has seven to eight irregular,
octofasciatum. faint, transverse bars on each flank. At spawning time the fish are
aggressive and quarrelsome. They need tanks with no vegetation so that
they have enough space for 'excavation work' in the substrate. The
male is usually larger than the female and has a fatty bump of varying
size on the front of the head. The egg yield per spawnings is 700 to 800.
The best temperature for breeding is 25° C. The parents take care of their
young together. The fry are not difficult to rear and if fed live 'powder'
food they grow rapidly. The sexes can be distinguished at the age of
one year when the fishes are 10—12 cm long. The Eight-banded Cichlid
lives up to five years in the aquarium.

Fire-mouth Cichlid (211) inhabits the waters of Guatemala and the Yucatan. It grows up to
Cichlasoma meeki 15 cm long. The males have strongly elongated dorsal, caudal and anal
fins. They often show off to each other by lifting their gill covers. The
pairs spawn most commonly in a stone cave or in a lying flower pot.
Both parents undertake the brood-care together. For some time after

196

spawning the young still stay in a shoal with their parents. The best breeding temperatures are from 24 to 26° C. Water in which the adults are kept should not drop below 20° C, in temperature.

Brown Discus or **Yellow-brown Discus** (212) comes from the waters of Brazil and grows to the length of 12—15 cm. It is hard to breed and rear in captivity. Both young and adults have rigid requirements for water quality, clean and varied food, and for cohabitants. It is recommended that this species be kept alone. They often suffer from diseases which are hard to treat with success. The fry need very careful attention from hatching to sexual maturity. During the first few days after hatching the fry feed on a dermal secretion produced by their parents and only later do they start eating normal 'powder' food. If the parents do not start producing the dermal secretion in time the young die. Some success has been recorded with the use of food replacers in recent years but such feeding is difficult, complicated and very time-consuming.

Symphysodon aequifasciata axelrodi

212

Some species and subspecies have been successfully crossed in captivity. Very hardy progeny were obtained from the hybridization of the Brown Discus *(Symphysodon aequifasciata axelrodi)* with the Red Discus *(Symphysodon discus)*. The latter comes from the Río Negro and its tributaries. It grows to the length of about 20 cm. It is even more difficult to keep than the Brown Discus.

Blue Discus (213) is known to inhabit the Amazon basin and the areas of Leticia and Benjamin Constant. Except for the middle part of the flanks the whole body of the fish is crossed with brilliant blue wavy bars which also cover the dorsal and anal fins. The head is decorated likewise. The iris of the eye is bright red. In Europe the Blue Discus has been successfully bred and

*Symphysodon
aequifasciata
haraldi*

213

214

reared in captivity for several years. It occasionally cross-breeds with the Brown Discus. The naturally occurring species, the Red Discus *(S. discus)*, the Green Discus *(S. aequifasciata)* and its subspecies, the Brown Discus *(S. ae. axelrodi)* and the Blue Discus *(S. ae. haraldi)*, enjoy high popularity among aquarists.

Newly discovered wild forms or artificially developed strains are also popular and they are marketed under commercial names such as 'Royal Blue Discus' and 'Cobalt Blue Discus', etc.

Blue Acara (214, 215) comes from Panama, Colombia, Venezuela and Trinidad. The size of the
Aequidens pulcher adult is 15 to 20 cm long. It is a deep-bodied fish, with five to eight black, transverse bars. A shining blue spot decorates each scale. At spawning time the body colours become richer. The male has longer anal and dorsal fins than the female. The breeding tanks should be large and the fish provided with plenty of food. The water must be kept clean, well-filtered and replaced frequently, since in old and turbid water the fish suffer from various diseases. The Blue Acara spawns several times a year. Although it is comparatively large, it does not stir up the substrate or destroy the plants. As in the majority of large cichlids,

frays often occur between the male and female; they hold each other's lips, and locked together, they push and pull each other. However, the 'fight' is soon over. The female cleans the spawning stone with great care. The brood number is high, and often numbers more than 1,000 young. At first the eggs are laid in a star pattern (215) but later the stone becomes covered uniformly with eggs laid close to each other. The female fans the eggs by movements of the pectoral fins and sometimes by twisting her body above them. Having learned to swim the young keep close to the parents in a shoal. If the tank is not large enough or if the parents are frequently disturbed it is wise to remove the young to a separate tank after some time. The fry readily devour any live 'powder' food immediately after they start to swim freely. They are not choosy and grow rapidly. Outside the spawning period the water can be about 24°C but in the spawning season it should be 26°C. The young reach sexual maturity at the age of eight to ten months when they are 7—8 cm long. Longevity is a characteristic feature of this species; some individuals live up to 10 years. They can be kept with fish of the same kind or with cichlids of adequate size with similar requirements for water purity.

217

Flag Cichlid (216) comes from the Amazon basin and grows to about 8 cm long. It is a peaceful
Aequidens curviceps   fish which can be kept in community tanks outside the breeding season.
The young breeding pairs usually devour the eggs from the first spawn-
ing after a day or two. Further spawnings are normal and the parents
take exemplary care of their eggs and young. The Flag Cichlid belongs
to the lithophilous species; that is, it spawns on flat stones. Before
spawning the parents carefully clean the stone with their mouths. The
female lays the eggs alone; then she leaves the stone to let the male
fertilize them. The female has a thick tubular or cylindrical ovipositor,
whereas the urogenital papilla of the male is conical and pointed. The
number of eggs laid on a stone gradually increases. The male swims
around the female and keeps any uninvited guests away. Both parents
share equally the protective duty and can replace each other in all
post-spawning functions. The best rearing temperature is 26°C. The
tank should be of medium size and have a sandy bottom. Both parents
dig pits for their spawn in the sand and water plants may be damaged
by this activity. The fish need live food of all kind and of adequate size
throughout their life.

Red Cichlid or **Jewelfish** (217, 218, 219, 220) lives in large populations in the drainage basins of
Hemichromis   the Nile, Congo and Niger Rivers. It inhabits fresh as well as brackish
bimaculatus   waters. The adult individuals are about 15 cm long. The male is larger
than the female. The back of the fish is olive to grey-brown with yellow-green flanks and a yellowish belly. At spawning time this fish is
perhaps the most splendid African cichlid. The male takes on a rich red

203

218

colour with shining green dots all over the body. The front part of the body of some females is sulphur yellow and the back part is red. In other populations the females are bright red all over the body (217). The pair spawn on stones. The male (218) and female alternately clean the stone on which the eggs are to be laid. The fish take curious positions during this work; they stand on their heads and attack the stone as if testing its strength.

Both parents take exemplary care of the eggs (219) and fry. The fry are very hardy. However, they cannot be kept together with any other species of cichlids since the young Red Cichlids are voracious and aggressive and harass the young of other species. They can survive high nitrite levels, unlike other fish which cannot prosper in such an environment. A large tank is needed for breeding Red Cichlids. They are quite unsuitable for community tanks. Older specimens must be kept separately or at most in pairs owing to their aggressiveness. Only highly resistant plants can be grown in the Red Cichlid tanks. The lower parts of these plants must be protected by stones. The bottom should be left bare or covered with pebbles or larger flat stones. Outside spawning time the water temperature can be kept at 20°C. In the rearing season the temperature should be increased to 25—26°C. Red Cichlids need only live food. Despite its incompatibility and aggressiveness, the Red Cichlid is popular among aquarists.

Borelli's Dwarf Cichlid (221) inhabits the South American territories of Mato Grosso and the
Apistogramma Río Paraguay basin to Argentina. It grows to a length of about 7.5 cm.
borellii The male (221) is larger than the female. The fish is very thermophilous
and water temperature should never be lower than 22°C. In smaller
aquariums the fishes spawn in separate pairs, whereas in its natural
habitat and in larger tanks the fish probably spawn in groups. The
young males always keep with a single female whereas the older males
spawn with several females at the same time and defend a territory
which would otherwise belong to more pairs. According to Wickler the
older males do not treat the young males as rivals but only protect
their territory against outside attacks.

Breeding and rearing of the young is fairly difficult. The younger
parents sometimes swallow the first few broods of eggs. At a temperature of about 26°C the young emerge within two to four days. After

221

another five to six days they consume all the nutritive yolk and start swimming freely. They associate in a shoal, keeping close to the female for some two to four weeks. At first the young should only be given fine live food such as rotifers but later they can be offered *Cyclops* nauplii and adult *Cyclops* and *Daphnia*. They grow quickly. A serious breeder does not leave the care of the young to the female but removes the eggs to separate, all-glass tanks; the fry emerge under artificial conditions with intensive aeration and filtration of the water.

Yellow Dwarf Cichlid (222, 223, 224) lives in the waters of the central part of Paraguay. The
Apistogramma   adults grow to about 5 cm long. The male, which is larger than the
reitzigi   female, has huge dorsal and anal fins. The back of the fish is green-grey, the flanks are grey-yellow and the belly is bright yellow. If the

207

224

fish are content, their body sides have a bluish sheen. Numerous bright green spots and streaks are scattered on the gill cover behind the eye. The males often display by spreading their fins but they never fight. These fish are best bred in soft water with slightly alkaline reaction at a temperature of about 26°C. The brood number is small; some 40—70 large and oval eggs are laid and these are pale brick red in colour. The brood-care instinct is highly developed in this species. If the eggs yield no fry or the female loses her young, another female's young can be given to her care instead; sometimes she will even take care of a shoal of daphnia given to her as food. The male must be removed after spawning.

In aquaristic classification the genus *Apistogramma* belongs among the so-called small cichlids. It comprises numerous species and the methods of keeping and breeding them are roughly the same. About 15 species have been imported in the last few decades. The following are most popular among aquarists: Agassiz' Dwarf Cichlid *(A. agassizi)*, Corumba Dwarf Cichlid *(A. commbrae)*, *A. kleei*, *A. ornatipinnis*, Ortmann's Dwarf Cichlid *(A. ortmanni)*, *(A. pertense)*, *A. sweglesi* and *A. trifasciatum haraldschultzi.*

Ramirez' Dwarf Cichlid (225, 226) is a popular aquarium fish coming from the Río Apure and
Papiliochromis Río Meta in Venezuela. The male is larger than the female and grows
ramirezi to be about 7 cm long. As distinct from the fish of the genus *Apistogramma,* the body of Ramirez' Dwarf Cichlid is deep and strongly
compressed on the sides. *Papiliochromis ramirezi* represents an intermediate form between the genera *Apistogramma* and *Geóphagus;* the
structure of its eggs is similar to those of the latter whereas the remaining characteristics are similar to those of the genus *Apistogramma.*
The main difference between the genera *Apistogramma* and *Papiliochromis* is in the position of the lateral line. The ground colour of Ramirez' Dwarf Cichlid is purple and changes by incident light. The flanks,
including the fins, are covered with shining green to blue spots. The
upper part of the iris is a brilliant light blue, the front part of the dorsal

225

fin is deep black. The first three spinous dorsal fin rays of the male are
markedly elongated. Breeding and rearing are similar to that in species
of the genus *Apistogramma.*

The breeding pairs prefer stones as the spawning place, but a pit in
the sand may serve just as well. Brood care is undertaken alternately
by both parents. A spawning yields 150—200 eggs. *P. ramirezi* is a beautiful fish but unfortunately it does not live long and usually dies within
two years. It requires clean water and suffers from many incurable
diseases, such as dropsy and fish tuberculosis. Its albino cultivated
strain (226), which has the same requirements as the original wild type,
has become popular in recent years.

Papiliochromis ramirezi

227

Golden-eyed Dwarf Cichlid (227, 228) is a native of western Guyana. The male is larger than
Nannacara anomala the female and grows to a length of about 8 cm. The male's body is
green in colour with a metallic lustre and a triangular spot on each
scale. The adults prosper best in richly planted tanks with many hiding
places under stones, roots and so on. They accept only live food, preferably in large pieces. Chironomid midge larvae and tubificid worms
are suitable. Outside the spawning season they are more or less com-
patible with fish of their own kind and with other species. The eggs are
laid on stones, into flower pots and in other places cleaned in advance.
After spawning the female undertakes all duties associated with brood
care. The male should be removed from the small space of the aquarium to avoid disturbing the female. Although she is always smaller than
the male, she may kill him in defence of the young. During brood-care
she takes on a characteristic colour. Her whole body bears a dark
lattice or net-like pattern which she retains for several weeks. At a water temperature of about 26°C the fry hatch within two to three days.

Nannacara anomala

212

228

The female immediately transfers them into a pit in the sand which she has made in advance. The fry start swimming freely after another five days. At first they accept live 'powder' food, which should be administered in frequent, small batches. Rearing requires intensive care only in the first days; later the fish are undemanding if kept in water of 24—25°C. The brood-care instinct is strongly developed in the females. It is touching to see a female which has lost her young take care of a cluster of daphnia or tubificid worms.

The Lattice Dwarf Cichlid *(N. taenia)*, which grows to a length of about 5 cm, is occasionally imported from countries in the Amazon basin. It has been successfully bred in captivity several times.

Badis (229) comes from the stagnant waters of India and grows to a length of about 8 cm. The
Badis badis male is usually larger than the female and his body is arched. The mouth of these fish is relatively small. *Badis badis* is the only species of the family Nandidae suitable for community tanks, as it is placid and

213

peaceful. It needs water temperatures between 26 and 28°C. The tank should provide hiding places under stones and roots, or dense thickets of aquatic plants. The fish accept all kinds of live food. In the spawning season the males display their outstretched fins and the dorsal fin is often erected. The eggs are laid in a hollow among stones or in a lying flower pot. The male takes care of the brood.

Oscar's or **Velvet Cichlid** (230) is a large cichlid coming from the waters of the Amazon, *Astronotus ocellatus* Paraná, Río Paraguay and Río Negro. It grows up to 35 cm long. The young have particularly splendid colours, marbled with chocolate brown in various shades with irregular black-edged markings. These 'youthful' colours disappear with increasing age and size, until a uni-

229

form brown-grey body colour is left. The tank must be large enough to suit the size of the fish. Oscar's Cichlid is unsuitable for a community tank. Every day it consumes a large amount of live food (flour worms, crickets, earthworms, pieces of lean beef, horse or poultry meat) in large pieces.

One spawning may yield more than 1,000 young which are carried about attached to the flanks of the parents during the first days of life.

214

230

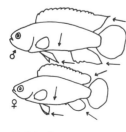

Badis badis

The young seek protection and perhaps also their first food, the dermal secretion, as in the discus fishes.

Owing to the wide distribution of the species, fish from different localities are differently coloured. Recently a splendid red strain known as the 'Red Oscar' has been artificially bred in aquariums and has aroused the interest of aquarists. Unlike the wild species, the adults are splendid red coloured specimens.

215

231

Congo Dwarf Cichlid (231, 232, 233) comes from the lower Congo. The male, which grows to
Nannochromis 8 cm long, is larger than the female. Soft water with a slightly acid
parilius reaction and moderate temperature (24—28°C) is the best environment for this fish. The males are quarrelsome and intolerant of each
other. The eggs are yellow in colour and oval in shape. The brood
numbers 80 to 120. After spawning the brood is attended by the female.
The fry hatch after about three days and begin to swim freely after
another three days. The results of breeding vary, are unpredictable
and probably depend on a number of unknown factors. Perhaps temperature, chemical composition of the water, food, and equipment of the
aquarium in which the pair breed are the most important factors.

Two other species, *N. dimidiatus* and *N. brevis* are also imported
from time to time and have similar requirements.

Pumpkinseed Sunfish (234) is a species of the family Centrarchidae; it is distributed in North
Lepomis gibbosus   America from Dakota to the Mexican Gulf. In the wild it grows to be
about 20 cm long; in aquariums it only grows to 10—12 cm. It has
acclimatized not only in aquariums but also in ponds and open waters;
e. g. in the drainage basins of the Danube and Elbe. The fish builds
dish-like pits in sand, which is the best spawning substrate. It is able to
survive the winter in unheated aquariums without difficulty. The fish
accept only live food. Breeding and rearing are simple.

Maria's Tilapia (235) is distributed in west Africa, mainly in the lower basin of the Niger and in
Tilapia mariae   Lagos. It grows to the length of about 15 cm. It is exclusively herbivorous in its natural habitat, where it eats stands of aquatic plants. It
spawns in hollows excavated by the females under stones. After about
two days the female picks the eggs from the ceiling of the crevice and
transfers them to a previously excavated pit made in sand. The young
emerge soon after this transfer. Having learned to swim, they feed on
live 'powder' food. The breeding temperature should be kept between
25 and 27°C.

Chromidotilapia kingsleyae (236) comes from southern Gabon and the adults are up to 25 cm
long. The eggs develop in a throat sac in the male's mouth. Although it
is very similar to *Chromidotilapia guentheri* (below), the well-known
cichlid expert Thys van den Audenauerde considers them as two separate species. The picture shows a female.

219

237

Guenther's Cichlid (237) lives in virgin-forest and savanna brooks of west Africa from the
Chromidotilapia
guentheri
Gold Coast to the Cameroons. In the wild it grows up to 20 cm long; in
captivity it does not exceed 16 cm. The females are always smaller than
the males. The fish is quarrelsome and can only be kept in pairs. It is
very voracious and is not choosy. The male keeps the eggs in the throat
sac in the mouth. The pairs usually spawn in a crevice and then the
male picks up the eggs. The fry develop at a temperature of about
27°C for 12—14 days. One spawning yields up to 150 young. Freely
swimming fry seek shelter in the male's mouth when they are threat-
ened.

Descriptions and data concerning the behaviour of both partners
vary. Some authors claim that, under some circumstances, the male and
female alternately carry the eggs in their mouths.

African Blockhead (238, 239) comes from the rapids of the lower and middle reaches of the
Steatocranus
casuarius
Congo River. The male is larger than the female and grows to 9 cm
long. The male's head has a large cushion of adipose fat tissue on the
front. The fish, which have a reduced swimbladder, move by jumping
movements on the water bed. In the aquarium they are timid and are
quite peaceful outside the breeding season. The eggs are laid in cave-
like shelters, e. g. flower pots. The fish do not dig in the substrate or
destroy the vegetation. Initially, brood care is the task of the male but
at about three weeks after spawning the parents join forces to make
a pit in front of the crevice into which they transfer the progeny. The

220

238

parents hide their young in the crevice at night. The male defends a large nesting area of about 25 cm radius around the crevice. The recommended breeding temperature is 24—28°C. Water should be soft and rather acid, with pH ranging from 5.6 to 6.0. Adult fish are sensitive to increased contents of nitrites in the water and to oxygen starvation.

239

240

241

Herotilapia multispinosa (240, 241, 242) is native to Central America where it lives in the Managua Lake in Nicaragua and in the small rivers of Guatemala, Panama and Costa Rica. The male grows to a length of about 12 cm and its belly is flat; in this it differs from the female which is smaller and has a rounded belly. The spawning season lasts three to four months and the fish lay 800—1,000 eggs at three to four week intervals. The eggs are tough and orange. If laid on glass they can be removed with a razor blade and transferred to an all-glass tank for further development without great losses. Spawning follows after courtship dis-

242

plays, preferably at 24—27° C. The breeding pairs seek the darker places of the tank for spawning. They stick the eggs to stones, into a flower pot or coconut shell, onto plant leaves, or on the glass wall of the tank just above the bottom. Picture 242 shows a male over the eggs. Water should be slightly acid (pH = 6) and with a hardness of up to 15° dGH. The parents incessantly clean the eggs with their mouths and fan them with their fins. The fry hatch after five days and the parents transfer them into a pit in the sand. They begin to swim freely within another period of five days. At this stage the parents can be removed and the young fish can be given 'powder' food.

If the water is kept pure, the young grow quickly up to a length of 1.5 cm. Their growth then markedly slows down. The characteristic body colouring (241) appears when the fish is about 5 cm long (at the age of six months). It reaches sexual maturity at the age of about nine months. Pronounced transverse bars indicate deterioration of health which may be due to long-lasting exposure to low temperatures (under 20° C).

223

243

Five-spot African Cichlid (243, 244) lives in large populations in the fresh and brackish waters
Thysia ansorgei of Nigeria, Ghana and the Ivory Coast. The adult male is larger than
the female and reaches a length of about 13 cm. Best breeding results
have always been obtained from those pairs which left the shoal by
themselves. They prefer to spawn into flower pots, on overhanging
slate plates or coconut shells. Both parents share duties of caring for
the brood. The eggs are large and light brown in colour. The young

hatch after three days and begin to swim freely after seven days. The water temperature should be about 26°C. Live and artificial food can be given to these fish.

The names *Pelmatochromis annectens* and *P. arnoldi* may also be encountered in literature, but these are scientifically invalid synonyms. In picture 243 the female is laying the eggs, in picture 244 the male is fertilizing them.

Red Dwarf Cichlid or **Kribensis** (245, 246) is a native of the tropical waters of west Africa and *Pelvicachromis pulcher* the estuary of the Niger delta. The male grows up to a length of 10 cm, the female only to 7 cm. The water temperature must be kept at 25—28° C for successful breeding. Adult specimens require a supplement of vegetable food in their diet. The parents share the brood care. They like to hide their eggs in shelters such as a flower pot. The eggs are red-brown in colour. A careful breeder transfers the eggs to all-glass tanks with slightly aerated water.

The fry hatch within two to three days and learn to swim in another four to five. If the aquarium does not offer suitable hiding places the fish build shelters under stones and among the roots of plants. They are incompatible with other fish of their own kind and should be kept in separate pairs. The species *P. pulcher* has two colour mutations known to aquarists under the names *P. kribensis* and *P. aureocephalus.* The sexes can easily be distinguished; the male's caudal fin is lanceolate whereas the caudal fin of the female is straight-edged.

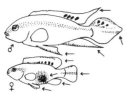

Pelvicachromis pulcher

245

Other species of the genus *Pelvicachromis* are also popular. *P. sub-ocellatus* and *P. taeniatus* are splendidly coloured and are very popular among aquarists. Breeding and rearing are basically the same in all species.

Orange Chromide (247, 248, 249) inhabits the fresh and brackish waters of south India and *Etroplus maculatus* Ceylon. It grows up to 8 cm long. In aquariums it is very sensitive to any change of water. It is frequently attacked by external parasites, particularly by *Ichthyophthirius multifiliis.* Treatment is difficult because the Orange Chromide is very sensitive to chemicals and drugs. Heavy infection by ichthys kills the fish. Some resistance to the disease is obtained if 1—2 teaspoons of sea salt per 10 litres of water are added to the aquarium. In tanks with adult specimens the temperature of the water should be no lower than 25°C. The fry should not be kept in water colder than 27°C. Reproduction is the same as in all lithophilous cichlids. The eggs are laid on stones (248). The brood care is undertaken jointly by the female and the male. After hatching, the fry remain attached to the parents for some time, as in discus. However the young fish can also be reared separately, if fed live 'powder' food of adequate size. Hence the fry do not depend entirely on the dermal secretion of their parents. The close mother/fry relationship (249) usually lasts a long time.

Cichlids on the Asian continent are represented only by one genus, *Etroplus,* with two species. The other species, the Green Chromide (*E. suratensis),* is also well-known among European aquarists who have

227

248

been keeping it since 1905. It comes from the brackish waters of Ceylon where it grows to 40 cm in length. Its ground colour is grey-green to blue-grey, with a beautiful nacreous lustre all over the body. Six to eight dark transverse bars cover the flanks. In fresh water this species can only be kept for a short time. However, pure sea water is also harmful to the fish, although it enhances the colours. The Green Chromide is thermophilous and requires constant temperatures above 23°C. Although it has not yet been reproduced in captivity, it is still very popular and is continuously exported. In aquariums it usually grows to a length of 12—15 cm. Sex distinctions are unknown.

250

Haplochromis burtoni (250) inhabits the tropical waters of east and central Africa and the northern reaches of the Nile basin. Adults grow up to a length of 12 cm. Confrontations between the partners are common during the courtship displays if the eggs of the female are still unripe. It is therefore useful to provide numerous shelters and hiding places in which the weaker female can escape from the attacks of the male which is eager to spawn. The optimal breeding temperature is 27°C. The pair needs plenty of live food, tubificid worms, larvae of chironomid midges and so on. This species has a very interesting method of securing complete fertilization of the eggs. Before the female lays the eggs the male lies on his side on a cleaned stone. He bends his body and ejects the milt while shivering all over. The female approaches with her head to the male's anal fin and tries to pick the egg-like colour pattern (250) from the fin while she sucks the sperm into her mouth. Then she lays a small batch of eggs on a stone and takes them into her mouth (the throat sac)

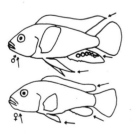

Haplochromis burtoni

230

251

and sucks the male's milt again. The whole process of spawning lasts about one and half hours. At water temperatures of 26 to 27°C, the eggs develop for sixteen to twenty days in the female's throat sac. Fully developed fry then leave the mother's mouth. The female offers the young the shelter of her mouth in time of danger and at night. This behaviour lasts for a period of about a week.

Similar breeding habits can be also observed in other African mouthbrooders, e. g. *H. desfontainesi* which is distributed all over north Africa.

Thomas's Dwarf Cichlid (251) comes from Africa, from the region of Kenema in Sierra Leone.
Pelmatochromis thomasi   The male, which grows up to 10 cm long, is larger than the female. In its general appearance this species resembles *Papiliochromis ramirezi.* Its body colours are splendid and very variable. The adult males are grey-green and have a shining blue mark on each scale. Three dark

231

252

blotches, one on the gill cover, another in the middle of the flanks and a third at the base of the tail complement the body colours of the fish. The blotches are indistinct on the flanks and give way to seven transverse bars, the first of which crosses the eye obliquely. The dorsal fin is fringed with red and has a shining golden margin. The upper lobe of the caudal fin is also rimmed with red. In the male the dorsal and anal fins are strongly produced and the pelvic fins have blue or black leading edges. *P. thomasi* lays green-grey eggs on a flat stone which has been cleaned in advance. The brood number is about 500 eggs. This undemanding African cichlid is content in water of 23—25°C but higher temperatures may speed up the development of the eggs and young. At 28°C the fry hatch within 48 hours and begin to swim freely after another three days. The young, which eat live 'powder' food, are easy to rear.

Southern Mouthbreeder (252, 253, 254) is a cichlid widely distributed in south-west Africa, in *Pseudocrenilabrus philander dispersus* the Transvaal, Rhodesia, Angola and Katanga. The male, which grows up to 11 cm long, is larger than the female. Water temperatures between 24 and 26° C are needed for breeding. Adult specimens, however, survive temperatures as low as 20°C. They prosper best in fresh, medium-hard water of a neutral reaction. To prevent the male from killing the female at spawning time the female must be carefully chosen and trouble is avoided if the female is filled with eggs and ready to spawn. The eggs are laid into a small pit which has been made in the sand by the male. After fertilization the female picks the eggs into her throat sac in which they can be seen as they get darker, particularly in the latter stages of the development (253). It is recommended that the male be removed immediately after spawning to prevent him from disturbing the female. The development of the eggs in the female's mouth lasts 10—12 days. The fry which leave the mother's mouth are about

6 mm long. They are immediately able to swim and seek food. At night, or in times of danger, the young find refuge in their mother's mouth. While she keeps the young in her mouth the female does not eat; she moves slowly, breathes with difficulty and is shy. The number of eggs laid at each spawning depends on the size of the female and ranges between 30 and 100. Rearing is easy. The young reach maturity at seven months.

Pseudotropheus auratus (255) is a native of the rocky coast of Lake Nyasa in the tropics. The male, which is larger than the female, grows up to the length of 11 cm. The male's ground colour is brown-black to blue-black; the female's is golden yellow with longitudinal bars. The body colours of this fish are very pronounced and conspicuous. The fish feed on algae and supplement this diet with tubificid worms and *Daphnia.* The female hatches the eggs in her mouth. Fully developed young, 1 cm long, leave their mother's mouth after 22—26 days. The number of young is small and ranges between 6 and 40.

Pseudotropheus zebra (256) is also a native of Lake Nyasa, but is larger than the preceding species; the male grows up to 15 cm long. It likes to stay among rocks in its natural environment and among stones in the aquarium. It is an omnivorous species which feeds not only on algae but on all kinds of food. It acclimatizes easily to aquarium conditions. The fish of this species are quarrelsome and each specimen occupies a comparatively large territory in nature. This implies that they are only suitable for large aquariums. The female hatches the young in her mouth.

Two other representatives of the genus *Pseudotropheus*, *P. elongatus* and *P. novemfasciatus*, are also kept by many aquarists. The latter makes an attractive showpiece for public aquariums.

Banded or **Yellow Julie** (257) lives in the rocky and stony littoral zone of Lake Tanganyika. The male grows up to about 8 cm long and is larger than the female. The fish is easy to keep in captivity in hard water of alkaline reaction. It also reproduces readily. The breeding pairs spawn in various narrow hollows and crevices among stones, often attaching the eggs to the ceilings of small holes. A coconut shel or a flower pot may suffice if there are no better spawning places. Brood care is undertaken mainly by the female, leaving the male to defend the outside of the nesting territorium. If danger threatens the male tries to block access to the female and the brood. The number of eggs at each spawning is small (usually not more than 20).

Julidochromis ornatus

Aquarists also keep the species *J. regani*, *J. transcriptus* and *J. marlie-*

257

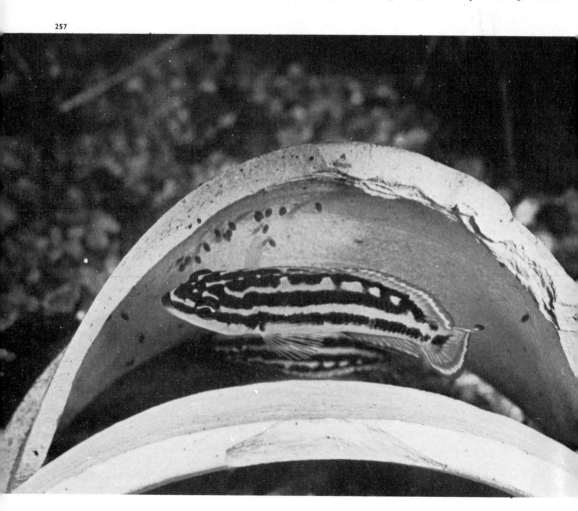

ri. The latter readily crosses with *J. ornatus* but the progeny is apparently infertile.

Lamprologus brichardi (258) comes from Lake Tanganyika and from rivers flowing into it. It lives in both shallow waters and depths of up to 10 m. The adult specimens are up to 9—10 cm long. In captivity about 50 litres of water will suffice for one pair. More than a pair of adults cannot be kept together, since they would quickly kill one another while pairing or protecting their young. They tear up the larger fish and swallow the smaller ones. Water for this species should be neutral to slightly alkaline at 26—28° C. Throughout their life the fish prefer fine-grade food, especially nauplii of brine shrimp. They refuse artificial foods. They love crystal clean water with a rocky bed and like to shelter in crevices. A tank shaded by tall plants may also give a good environment for this

237

259

species. The breeding pairs live in harmony. The red eggs are laid in the dark of crevices and are stuck onto the ceiling. The brood number is 30 to 200 eggs. The eggs are guarded carefully by the parents and emerge after some 10—12 days. The spawning season lasts about two months, in the course of which the breeding pairs spawn several times. The larger young are indifferent to their smaller siblings but the parents take the same care of all generations. Nevertheless, it is still advisable to separate the young from the parents after two months. The fry grow slowly. They prosper best when fed nauplii of brine shrimp.

Ring-tailed Pike Cichlid (259) occurs in large populations in Trinidad and in the central and *Crenicichla saxatilis* eastern part of the Amazon basin to southern Brazil. In the wild it grows to 35 cm long. In captivity it is much smaller. The tanks for spawning should be as large as possible. The breeding pairs spawn in shallow pits in sand. The brood care is the male's task but the females need not be removed. The whitish eggs are very small. The adult fishes greedily devour small fish, larvae of dragon-flies, various water worms and pieces of lean meat. Water temperature should not drop below 20°C.

Melanochromis brevis (260) comes from Lake Nyasa and does not grow to more than 6—7 cm in length. It is quarrelsome but skirmishes never lead to serious injuries.

260

The ground colour is glossy brown with a bluish sheen. The males have a marked orange blotch on their anal fin. The aquarium should be large, holding 50 litres or more, and the bottom should be rocky. The fish must be kept in crystal clear, hard and alkaline water at temperatures of 25—28°C. Young and adults are very sensitive to pH values under 7 and to increased contents of nitrites in the water. They need live food, but pieces of meat, or TetraMin and TetraPhyll are also accepted. Spawning females are easily recognized by the sacs on the lower part of their mouths. Such females should be carefully trans-

239

261

262

240

ferred to a small glass tank with intensive aeration. The separated females should not be given any food because they cannot eat with their brood in the mouth. The eggs develop for about 17 days. The young are very shy at first and quite independent. The fry are about 8 mm. The colour of the fry is the same as that of the adults. Rearing is simple and easy.

Nandus (261, 262) belongs to the family Nandidae and comes from India, Burma and Thailand.
Nandus nandus   The size of full-grown individuals is about 20 cm. This species is very predaceous, both in the wild and in captivity. The mouth is very large and protractile (261) enabling the fish to 'suck in' the prey. It is best kept in slightly brackish water by adding 1—2 teaspoons of sea salt per 10 litres of water. The fish is frequently imported but has not yet been successfully bred in captivity.

Eartheater or **Demon Fish** (263) lives in waters with sandy bottoms in the Amazon basin and in
Geophagus jurupari   Guyana. It associates in shoals and the individuals grow up to the length of 23 cm. Despite their 'hostile' appearance the fish of this species are peaceful. They do not dig in the substrate and do not destroy well rooted plants. Both in the wild and in captivity they keep chewing the detritus from the bottom soil, taking anything edible. The Eartheater prefers food of a small size, such as *Daphnia,* tubificid worms and larvae of chironomid midges. Even during winter the temperature in the tank should be kept at 22°C. The fish prospers best at 25—28°C since it is a thermophilous species. Eggs are deposited on a stone. The parents take care of them for a day, then take them in their mouths where they remain until they hatch.

The Eartheater represents an intermediate between cichlids which

263

241

264

brood their eggs in a sand pit and the true mouth-brooders. Swimming fry return to their parents' mouths from time to time during the first two weeks of life.

The genus *Geophagus* includes many other species. Most of them are quarrelsome and great diggers. In some of them brood care is similar to that described for species in the genus *Cichlasoma*. Others are mouth-brooders or take their young into their mouth in times of danger. They are distributed throughout South America, as far south as the river La Plata. *Geophagus gymnogenys* and *G. australe* withstand temperatures as low as 12—15°C.

The small *G. cupido,* about 13 cm long, is a typical mouth-brooder. The three warmth-loving species, *G. surinamensis, G. acuticeps* and *G. brasiliensis* are giants among geophages; they grow to a length of 25—30 cm. They establish and defend their own territories and are quarrelsome and intolerant if they do not have enough shelter. All species feed mainly on various plant remains.

Labidochromis coeruleus (264) comes from Lake Nyasa. In captivity it grows to a length of 7—8 cm. It is quarrelsome but skirmishes do not lead to serious wounds in either party. The water in the tank should be crystal clear, hard and alkaline, free from nitrites and warm (25—28°C). The males are azure blue and their pelvic fins are conspicuously long and are bordered with black. The orange blotches on the anal fin are much more pronounced in the females than in the males. The blotches are even absent from some males. The females are much smaller, inconspicuous and grey-blue. The eggs are brooded in the female's mouth. Breeding is similar to that of *Melanochromis brevis*. The eggs develop for about 20 days and the young leaving their mother's mouth are 1 cm long, independent and they tend to escape from the mother. The brood number is low. The fry should be fed with live 'powder' food. Rearing them is easy.

Limnochromis auritus (265) is a native of Lake Tanganyika where it grows to a length of about 19 cm. It is peaceful and shy. The water should be crystal clear, hard, alkaline and warm (25–28°C). The fish eats any live food, preferably large pieces of earthworms or meat. In the wild it lives in depths from 5 to 125 metres. In captivity the activity of the fish increases at dusk. During the day they spend most of their time hidden in shelters among stones. Although fish of this species remain voracious in captivity, their health deteriorates after a long time and all attempts to breed them have so far failed.

Basket-mouthed Cichlid (266) comes from the waters of Guyana and northern parts of the
Acaronia nassa Amazon basin. The adults grow up to 20 cm long. Until 1940 it was included in the genus *Acaropsis*, but Myers found that the generic name had already been used for another animal and erected a new genus for this fish *(Acaronia)* which now includes the species *A. nassa* and *A. trimaculata*.

  Acaronia nassa is quarrelsome and a great biter and can only be

266

kept with other predators of the same size and of the same quarrelsome temper. The tank must be as large as possible. Cohabiting individuals of the same species are tolerant and comparatively peaceful only if they have plenty of hiding places among stones or under roots, or if individual fishes can defend their territory. Attacks are short and are mainly aimed at defending their shelter. Water temperature in which this species is kept should never drop below 22°C. The fish eat any living food but prefer small fish. Reproduction in captivity has not yet been observed, although European aquarists have kept this species since 1909. Imports are irregular.

Chapter 7

THE FOAMY CRADLE FOR THE YOUNG

Labyrinth fishes (Anabantidae) are widely distributed in fresh water of south-eastern Asia and in the tropical zone of Africa. They are believed to have evolved from the same ancestors as the perches. Anabantids have become adapted to life in shallow, often muddy waters which are usually poor in oxygen. To survive in such an unfavourable environment they have a labyrinth, an accessory respiration organ, which enables them to obtain atmospheric oxygen.

The body of these fish is covered with ctenoid scales. The dorsal and anal fins are supported by spines in the front parts. At spawning time some of the labyrinth fish build a foam nest just beneath the water surface or deeper in the water under the leaves of aquatic plants. This nest, into which the eggs are deposited, is built from air bubbles which are surrounded by a hardened secretion from the oral mucous membrane. The male undertakes the care of the brood alone. Many species are successfully kept and reproduced in aquariums.

Three-spot Gourami (267, 268, 269) comes from the Malay Peninsula, Thailand, South Vietnam, *Trichogaster trichopterus* and the Greater Sunda Islands. It grows up to 15 cm. It includes many colour varieties. The most popular among them is the Blue Gourami *(Trichogaster trichopterus sumatranus)* (269) from Sumatra which is variable in colour; the cultivated strains are golden (267, 268), silver or marbled and are known under the commercial name *T. trichopterus* 'Cosby', after the successful breeder who initiated and stabilized this form. The wild form of the Three-spot Gourami is less demanding for warmth than all its splendidly coloured cultivated strains. Apart from this the main requirements for care in captivity are generally the same in all forms. They reach sexual maturity when about 7–8 cm long. The male drives the female before pairing and builds the foam nest just beneath the water surface. The fish constantly change their body colours during courtship. When the male feels that the nest is firm enough he tries to entice the female under the layer of bubbles. The female

267

with ripe eggs follows him and once under the nest the fish stop and stand side by side with their mouths somewhat raised. The female is embraced from the side and rotated onto her back (268). The fish then quiver for a moment and jerk abruptly, and a cloud of eggs and milt is ejected. After the act both fish fall towards the water bed. The eggs, which contain numerous oil droplets, ascend to the surface. The male collects the eggs and spits them into the nest. When spawning is over the male adds new layers of bubbles to the underside of the nest and drives the female away, sometimes vigorously. The female should therefore be cautiously removed at this stage to avoid disturbance of the male during brood care. The fry hatch after about three days at a water temperature of about 28°C. One spawning sometimes yields more than

269

1,000 very small young. They should be fed with rotifers at first and nauplii of *Cyclops* in later stages of growth. The respiratory labyrinth does not develop in the young fish until the age of three to four weeks when they start breathing the air at the water surface. It is very important at this stage to keep the temperature under the covering glass the same as in the water otherwise the fry 'catch cold' and soon die.

Besides this species with beautiful cultivated strains, other gourami species are also kept in aquariums. Some of these are the Moonlight Gourami *(T. microlepis)* and the Snake-skinned Gourami *(T. pectoralis)*, which are far less splendid than all forms of the Three-spot Gourami. These two species spawn quietly and peacefully. The Snake-skinned

247

270

271

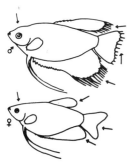

Trichogaster leeri

Gourami takes care of the young for a very long time and never attacks or threatens the fry of other fish, however small they may be.

Pearl or **Mosaic Gourami** (270, 271, 272, 273) comes from the waters of the Malay Peninsula, *Trichogaster leeri* Thailand, Sumatra and Borneo. It grows to a length of about 11 cm. It is very peaceful, shy and warmth-loving. At spawning time the male usually builds a large bubble nest which is wide and high. Spawning, breeding and rearing are generally the same as in the Three-spot Gourami.

It must be emphasized that the fishes of the genus *Trichogaster* must be given plenty of live food and that the composition of the diet must be varied. *Cyclops, Daphnia,* larvae of chironomid midges, gnats and mayflies are the best food. Long-continued feeding with tubificid worms, particularly in the winter season, often leads to fatalities. An unsuitable diet not only encourages the transmission of infections but may also support the development of infectious dropsy (the ulcerous form) and fish tuberculosis. Both diseases are hard to treat and sometimes kill large stocks which would be otherwise kept successfully.

249

Siamese Fighting Fish (274, 275, 276, 277, 278, 279) is widely distributed in the Malay Peninsula
Betta splendens and Thailand. The adults are up to 6 cm long. Populations from Siam
and Vietnam are mostly green; those from Singapore are red. The gill
cover of the Siamese Fighting Fish is always red. Long-finned forms of
various colours have been developed through artificial selection. At
spawning time the male builds a comparatively large nest, about
10×10 cm in size. The courtship displays take place near the nest and
are full of various splendid movements. The male displays the splendour of his outstretched fins. This display behaviour (275) lasts for
varying lengths of time, depending on readiness to spawn. Mating itself
takes place under the foam nest (276). The eggs ejected by the female
are heavier than water and slowly fall down to the bottom. Immediately after each spawning act the male picks up the eggs (277) and spits

273

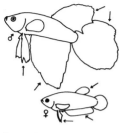

Betta splendens

them into the nest. The female often helps him. Later, the male drives her away from the nest. He continues adding further layers of bubbles to the nest from below, thus building the eggs into the nest. When spawning is complete the female must be removed, otherwise the male might bite her to death in the small space of the breeding tank. The fry hatch at a water temperature between 27 and 28°C within 24—36 hours, and are carefully tended by and protected by the male. They are best fed with live 'powder' food such as rotifers, nauplii of *Cyclops* and brine shrimp. Growth is rapid and at the age of five to six months the fish are fully developed and ready to reproduce.

In their native countries, the male Siamese Fighting Fish are used like cocks in cock-fights in public contests. In captivity numerous cultivated varieties of *Betta splendens,* differing in colour and shape, have

274

been developed. The most popular specimens combine the splendour of colouring with extremely well developed dorsal, caudal and anal fins. The caudal fin of the best quality male specimens should be as long as the rest of the body. Among all the colour varieties, emerald green with a metallic lustre, blue, red, yellow to dark green, dark blue, dark red, violet, or velvet black enjoy the highest popularity. Some aquarists also keep varieties with translucent fins (the so-called hyaline fighters), or with milk white fins. Combination of colour on both the fins and body (279) (in the so-called Singapore strains) are also known.

275

Some colour variants are stable, inherited from generation to generation, but others can only be perpetuated by continual crossing.

Apart from *B. splendens* other species of fighting fish of the genus *Betta* are kept in aquariums where they grow up to a length of 8—12 cm. The Slim Fighting Fish *(Betta bellica)*, Striped Fighting Fish *(Betta fasciata)* and *Betta smaragdina* have the same behaviour as the Siamese Fighting Fish. In the Javan Mouth-brooding Fighting Fish *(B. picta)*, Penang Mouth-brooding Fighting Fish *(B. pugnax)*, *B. brederi,*

B. taeniata and *B. anabantoides,* the brood care is the male's duty as in
the mouth brooders. The fry develop for 8—12 days, depending on the
species and on water temperature.

278

279

Pacific Fighting Fish (280) is found only in one locality in India and from the area of Kuala
Betta imbellis Lumpur where it was discovered as recently as 1970. It grows up to
5 cm. The gill cover is always green. This very shy labyrinth fish only
shows the splendour of its colours in a shaded tank in the company of
fish of its own kind. The males try hard to intimidate one another but
this never leads to serious injury. The spawning behaviour is the same
as in the Siamese Fighting Fish, but compared with the Siamese Fighting Fish which lays 500—800 eggs at one spawning, female Pacific
Fighting Fish will scarcely produce more than 200. The eggs of *Betta
imbellis* are large and the fry are robust but clumsy at the beginning,
feeding only on the finest grade and very slowly moving food such as
infusorians and rotifers. They are able to swallow the nauplii of *Cyclops*
and brine shrimps after four to six days of free swimming. Their growth

254

is also very slow. The young fish do not usually reach sexual maturity until eight to nine months. They require comparatively soft water up to about 6° dGH, carbonate hardness not exceeding 1° dCH and a neutral water pH value. In contrast to the Siamese Fighting Fish, which almost never jumps above the surface, *Betta imbellis* is a very good leaper and can jump as high as 20 cm above the water surface. If the tank is not tightly covered the fish literally crawls up the corners and passes through incredibly narrow slits between the edge of the tank and the cover glass.

The feeding habits of this species are also different; it does not throw itself greedily upon food, but approaches it reluctantly, turns it over in the mouth, spits it out and takes it again several times before swallowing it.

255

281

Dwarf Gourami (281, 282) comes from India. It grows to 5 cm long and is deep-bodied with
Colisa lalia   a splendid metallic lustre. The male's body is alternately covered with
oblique brown-red and green-blue transverse rows of tiny spots which
are fused into narrow bars extending to the unpaired fins. The whole
head and belly are dark blue-green. The ends of the caudal and anal
fins are brilliant red; the thread-like ventrals are orange-red. The female is smaller and paler. The male builds a large foam nest which is
supported by various available plant material, especially algae, plant
leaves, parts of *Myriophyllum* and tufts of *Vesicularia dubyana*. The
Dwarf Gourami is one of the loveliest of fish and is an aquarium favourite. However, it often suffers from skin parasites, *Amyloodinium* being
the most dangerous. Short and sharp sounds are produced during terri-
torial defence and in courtship displays. The fish can also spit water
over a short distance above the surface. At spawning time the water

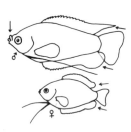

Colisa labiosa

256

temperature should be about 30°C. The breeding and rearing is similar to that of the Three-spot Gourami *(Trichogaster trichopterus).*

Thick-lipped Gourami (283) comes from southern Burma. The male, which is larger than the
Colisa labiosa female, grows up to a length of 8 cm. The eggs are kept in a nest on the water surface. They contain large quantities of fat which makes them float. Breeding and rearing are the same as in the Three-spot Gourami. Water temperature should be kept at 27—30°C. The male's dorsal fin has a red margin and the anal fin is rimmed with white. The body is strongly compressed from the sides.

Giant Gourami, Striped or **Banded Gourami** (284) is a close relative of the Thick-lipped
Colisa fasciata Gourami. It is a native of India and Burma where it lives in muddy waters and grows to a length of 12 cm. The water in the tank should be

283

kept at 24−28°C. Higher temperatures (up to 30°C) are recommended for spawning and for rearing the young. However, adult fish can withstand temperatures as low as 15°C. They are not choosy about food. The Giant Gourami differs from its thick-lipped relative in the whitish rim on the dorsal fin and red rim on the anal fin. Its body is cylindrical and elongated.

Colisa chuna (285) is a native of north-east India. It is the smallest of all the gouramis; its body is only 4−4.6 cm long. Many colour modifications of this species are known to exist due to its wide distribution in nature. In addition, a golden strain has been cultivated artificially. Breeding in captivity is simple. The pairs spawn at a comparatively low temperature of about 24°C. The brood number is small, ranging from 150 to 250 young. The fry must be fed the finest grade 'powder' food in the first one or two weeks. Perhaps rotifers are the best food since the youngest fish have

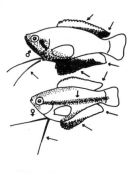

trouble in catching jumping *Cyclops* nauplii. Immature fish and females have a broad brown longitudinal band on their flanks which is a clear distinguishing feature.

Almost all *Colisa* species are very susceptible to disease (*Amyloodinium* and infectious dropsy). Like fish of the genus *Trichogaster*, species of *Colisa* are most susceptible to disease in winter when fed tubificid worms over a long period of time. *Colisa chuna* is an exception; it

can be fed tubificid worms throughout the year without any ill effect. However, it has difficulty swallowing *Daphnia* because of the tough indigestible chitin shell. The shells get stuck in the gourami's throat and the fish suffocate.

Black Paradise-fish (286, 287) is a native of Indochina where it grows to about 10 cm long. It is *Macropodus opercularis concolor* distinguishable because of its uniform dark colouring. The male has conspicuously developed dorsal, caudal and anal fins. The transverse bars on the body are black at spawning time and the fins are red. The caudal fin is greatly extended by many loose thread-like fin rays. The fish is peaceful in captivity. It requires exclusively live food. At spawning time the males are pugnacious and quarrelsome to one another. Black Paradise-fish readily cross with the initial form, the Paradise-fish *(M. opercularis opercularis),* and produce fertile progeny. The colour of the hybrids is dirty and unattractive.

286

Paradise-fish (288, 289, 290) comes from the waters of Korea, China, South Vietnam and Formosa. The male is up to 9 cm long. Water temperature of 15 to 20°C is sufficient for keeping this fish but for breeding the water should be warmer (20 — 24°C). The Paradise-fish is a quarrelsome species, unsuitable for community tanks. Fasted specimens are used by aquarists for controlling planarien-worms in the tanks.

Macropodus
opercularis
opercularis

A purebred red-eyed albino form (289, 290) has been known since the 1940's. Although it looks attractive in the tank, it has never been very popular among aquarists.

Paradise-fish fix their foam nests on the water surface among floating plants. Natural environments of irrigation canals overgrown with *Eichhornia crassipes* offer them many such localities for nesting. The Paradise-fish was the first fish to have been reproduced in captivity; this success was achieved by P. Carbonier in Paris at the end of the nineteenth century and the fish quickly became popular throughout

Macropodus opercularis
concolor

287

288

Europe. It is advisable to give the fish plenty of food immediately before spawning. The male builds the foam nest for several hours or days, depending on the partner's readiness to spawn. While working on the nest the male keeps driving the female away but when his work is finished he tries to entice her under the nest. He swims close to her, displays his outstretched fins and slowly returns to the nest, watching to see whether the female is following. If she is willing to spawn the two fish lie side by side, heads to tails with their heads turned slightly upwards and then they slowly turn until they become closely adpressed

to each other's flank. The male embraces the female and turns her upside down; both fish shiver for a moment and then a small cloud of eggs is ejected by the female (289). When the act is finished, both parents slowly fall to the bottom. The male is the first to recover and he collects the eggs and spits them into the foam nest. The spawning act is repeated many times at various intervals until the female has ejected all the ripe eggs. When spawning is complete the female should be removed as the male alone takes care of the brood. Rearing is similar to that of the Three-spot Gourami, with the exception that the Paradise-fish does not require such fine live 'powder' food.

Talking or **Croaking Gourami** (291, 292, 293) is native to the waters of Thailand, South
Vietnam, the Malay Peninsula and the Greater Sunda Islands. Its maximum length is 6.5 cm. The unpaired fins are long and pointed. Spawning in captivity is not easy. It can best be achieved in spring in a tank exposed to sunshine and overgrown with aquatic plants, in water kept at 28 to 30° C.

During courtship, the male gives off croaking sounds, probably produced with the aid of the labyrinth and the proximal part of swimbladder. Some authors claim that the female produces the same sounds.

Trichopsis vittatus

291

Dwarf Croaking Gourami (294) is smaller than its 'croaking' relation. It comes from South Vietnam, Thailand and Sumatra and only grows to 3.5 cm long. The nest takes the form of a small foam ball (it may sometimes be discoid) which is attached to the underside of a broad leaf, or made in a flower pot or coconut shell close to the bottom (10—15 cm above the water bed). The brood number is small, being up to 350 in the best fed specimens. The fry hatch at water temperatures between 27 and 28°C within about 36 hours. Many pairs spawn several times in succession, in short intervals of four to seven days. The Dwarf Croaking Gourami is another species in which the males croak during courting. The free swimming fry are large enough to be able to swallow brine shrimp nauplii from the start.

Trichopsis pumilus

292

293

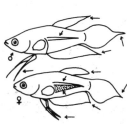

Trichopsis pumilus

Schaller's Gourami *(T. schalleri)*, which was found in Thailand and described in 1962 by Ladiges, has a similar appearance and the same breeding requirements.

Comb-tail Paradise-fish (295) comes from Ceylon and grows to a length of about 13 cm. It is
Belontia signata   a very pugnacious species. The sex distinctions are very inconspicuous. The male has longer dorsal and anal fins and the loosely projected rays of the male's caudal fin are also longer than those of the female. The female has a blotch at the end of the dorsal fin which is absent in the male. The best temperature for keeping this fish is 24 to 28°C. For reproduction the temperature should be 26—28°C. The eggs are 2—3 mm across and the female lays them into a foam nest under a float-

295

ing plant leaf. The foam nest sometimes consists of one large bubble. The fry hatch within 40—48 hours and begin to swim freely after another six days. The young are large and able to capture the nauplii of brine shrimp from the very beginning.

296

Sharp-nosed or **Marbled Climbing Perch** (296) is a native of the tributaries of the Lower Congo. It grows up to a length of 10 cm. It is quarrelsome, like the other species of the genus *Ctenopoma*, and is not suitable for community tanks. It needs plenty of vegetable food but it also greedily devours small fish. The breeding pairs spawn deep in the water at a temperature between 28 and 30°C. They do not build a foam nest. The eggs, which contain large quantities of fat, float on the surface. The fry retain their juvenile colour for some time, with the posterior part of the body remaining black.

Ctenopoma oxyrhynchus

Chapter 8   CURIOUS FRESHWATER FISHES

The fish described in this chapter are kept in freshwater aquariums all over the world. They come from every continent and represent 13 families but form just a fraction of the wide variety of species under these families. This means that it is difficult to list any common characteristics. The different species have found different ways of adapting to their natural environment and have developed interesting habits and modes of living. They may hatch their eggs in their mouths (although they are unrelated to cichlids); some of them leap over the water surface and glide on their broad pectoral fins, some shoot down flying insects with a drop of water. Others produce weak electric discharges for orientation and for marking their territory and some live a secretive life remaining buried in the substrate while others crawl and skip in the half-dried mud of river banks, hunting insects.

Arowana (297, 298) lives in the waters of the northern part of South America in Guyana and in the Amazon basin. It grows up to a length of 120 cm. Its dorsal and anal fin are long and are opposite each other. The fish of this species like to associate in shoals in stagnant and shallow waters in old river arms or in lakes. Their diet is extremely varied; they feed on any live food, from plankton to fish. The female keeps the eggs in her mouth until the young emerge, and in this resemble the behaviour of mouth-brooders. Two forked barbels on the lower jaw are a characteristic feature of this species. Figure 297 shows a young fish in which the barbels are relatively longer than in the adult. Young specimens are best suited for life in captivity. They need soft water enriched with peat extract and the temperature should be about 25°C. The smallest specimens greedily devour *Daphnia* and the larvae of gnats and many other water insects. When older, they prefer fish. Vegetable food may be added to their diet. Medium size specimens make beautiful exhibits for public aquariums. It is advisable to keep the tank well covered as this species is a good leaper.

Osteoglossum bicirrhosum

297

Primitive features are characteristic of the family Osteoglossidae. Fish of this family are close relatives of species of the family Arapaimidae, which includes the largest freshwater fish currently known — the South American *Arapaima gigas* which grows to as much as 2 to 4.5 metres.

Butterfly-fish (299) belongs to the family Pantodontidae and comes from west Africa, Congo, Niger and the Cameroons. The adult specimens grow to 10—15 cm long. This fish lives near the surface and is able to glide on its wide pectoral fins over a distance of 2 metres. Its pectoral fins often make flapping movements, resembling active flight. Its prey consists of insects living near the water. In the aquarium it should be given cockroaches, crickets, large flies, insect larvae and small fish. Soft water with

Pantodon buchholzi

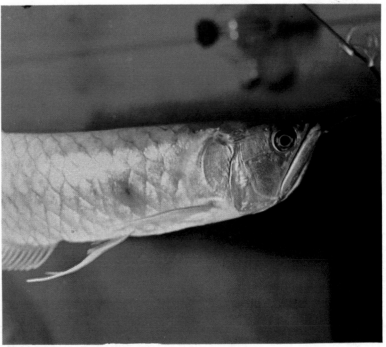

298

peat extract and temperatures between 25 and 30°C are recommended for breeding. During spawning the fish twist themselves around each other. The eggs are probably fertilized internally. They float on the water surface and the parents do not take care of them. The fry hatch within about three days. Breeding and rearing is difficult and success is never guaranteed.

Five-spined Archerfish (300) and four other archerfish species of the family Toxotidae live in the coastal regions of southern Asia, the Malay Peninsula, Indochina, the Philippines, and Australia. *T. chatareus* lives in freshwater as well as in the brackish waters of river estuaries. The adult specimens are about 27 cm long. They keep close to the surface and their back is

Toxotes chatareus

270

therefore straight. Like its smaller relative, the Archerfish *(T. jaculator)*, *T. chatareus* can spit a powerful jet of water at insects above the surface and bring them down from a distance of up to 150 cm. In captivity it prefers insect food such as flies, crickets and cockroaches. Older specimens are pugnacious to each other. Nothing is known about their reproduction. In their natural habitat the young have refractive flecks on the body. They like to associate in shoals but the older specimens prefer solitude.

Indian Freshwater Garfish (301) lives in waters in India, Ceylon, Burma, Thailand and the *Xenentodon cancila* Malay Peninsula. It grows up to 30 cm long. This species belongs to the family of garfishes (Belonidae) which is widely distributed in the open sea as well as in coastal waters. Only a few species enter river estuaries.

300

Xenentodon cancila is one of the species which are permanently adapted to life in fresh water. Its body is cylindrical and considerably elongated and the long and beak-like jaws bear a strong dentition. The pectoral and pelvic fins are small. The bases of the dorsal and anal fins are located opposite each other and are set very far back. The fish live near the surface. Fully grown specimens prefer fish and frogs as food. They are accomplished leapers and can jump almost vertically. They are suitable for large public aquariums. Reproduction in captivity has not yet been achieved.

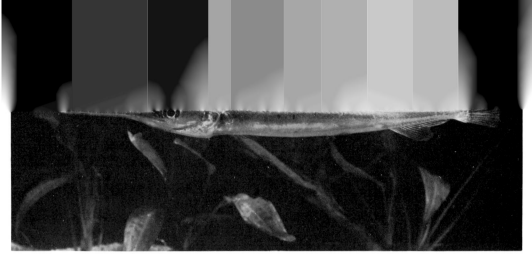

Green Knife-fish (302) is distributed throughout northern South America, southwards to La
Eigenmannia Plata. It grows up to a length of 45 cm. It has an unusual appearance
virescens because there are no dorsal, caudal or pelvic fins. The absence of these
fins is characteristic of all representatives of the South American knife-
fishes (Rhamphichthyidae). The function of these fins is performed by
a long anal fin which enables equally rapid forward and backward
movement. The fish requires no special care in captivity. It hides during
the day but is lively at dusk and at night. Green Knife-fishes greedily
devour the larvae of chironomid midges, earthworms, small fish and
pieces of lean meat. In captivity it soon loses its shyness but larger
individuals tend to be quarrelsome towards each other.

Their close relatives, species of the family Apteronotidae, e. g. *Aptero-
notus albifrons,* are known as pseudoelectric or slightly electric fish.
Their electric organs have probably developed from nerve cells and
are located on the ventral side of the body all along the long anal fin.
They usually extend from the pectoral fins or the head and reach to the
tip of the tail. The weak, high frequency electric discharges are produced continuously. There are electrical impulses probably used for

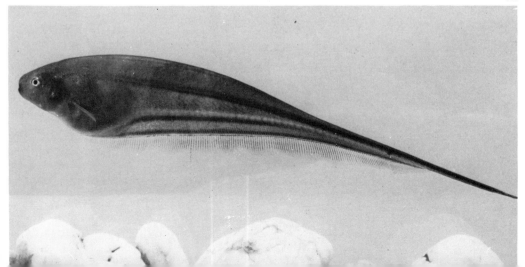

orientation as well as for delimiting the territory controlled by the fish.
fish.

African Knife-fish (303) is a representative of the family of African knife-fishes (Notopteridae).
Xenomystus nigri It is widely distributed from the estuary of the Nile to Liberia. The maximum length of adult specimens is 20 cm. The fish produces barking sounds by letting gas pass from the swimbladder to the digestive tract.

The African Knife-fishes are peaceful inhabitants of the weedy reaches of great rivers and stagnant backwaters in southern Asia and Africa. Their swimbladder functions as an accessory respiratory organ. At night they seek food on the bottom. They feed on insect larvae, worms, snails and small fish. Water for these fish should be soft and rather warm (25 to 28°C). The brood is deposited on the water bed, on

303

304

a stone, a piece of wood or in a pit in the sand. The eggs are guarded by one of the parents, usually the male. Young fish are suitable for the domestic aquarium. Adult specimens make interesting exhibits in public aquariums.

Spiny Eel (304) is distributed from India to the Malay Peninsula and the Molucca Islands. It *Macrognathus* lives in fresh and brackish waters and grows up to a length of 35 cm. *aculeatus* The females are larger than the males. In the aquarium it reaches sexual maturity when 12—15 cm long. In contrast to some related species its dorsal, caudal and anal fins are distinctly separate from each other. The fish hide during the day with their bodies buried in sand. Only in the evening and at night do they leave their hiding place. All suitably sized animals which can pass through their small mouths are devoured by this species. The tank should be planted with robust aquatic vegetation and stones, with pieces of wood on the bottom. The water should

275

305

be medium-hard and preferably slightly salted with kitchen or sea salt. Partial water replacement from time to time and good filtration are beneficial to these fish. *Macrognathus aculeatus* is peaceful and tolerant to other species and can be kept together with other placid fish.

Deep-bodied Spiny Eel (305) is a native of India and has been reproduced many times in captivity. The adults are up to 20 cm long. They spawn under the water surface into fine-leaved plants. The fry hatch after about three days and at first are suspended on water plants. After another three days they begin to swim freely and take the nauplii of brine shrimp. In the tank

Mastacembelus pancalus

306

they stay in the upper layers of the water until a size of about 3 cm is reached; then they adapt to benthic life on the water bed.

White-blotched Spiny Eel (306) lives only in Thailand. Its length is up to 25 cm. Reproduction in captivity has not yet been achieved.
Mastacembelus argus

The spiny eels (Mastacembelidae) inhabit the fresh and brackish waters of equatorial Africa and southern Asia. More than 30 species of the two genera, *Macrognathus* and *Mastacembelus,* are currently known. Besides the species described above, aquarists keep *Mastacembelus armatus, M. loennbergi, M. maculatus* and *M. laticauda.* Care in aquarium culture is about the same as in *Macrognathus aculeatus.*

Large Freshwater Pipefish (307) inhabits the lower courses of the Niger and Congo Rivers and prefers thickly weeded shallows in freshwater. It grows up to a length of 20 cm.
Microphis smithi

Pipefishes (Syngnathidae) have a typically elongated body which is hexagonal in cross section. The dorsal fin, when present, has only soft rays. Two nostrils can be seen on the sides of the head in front of the

307

eyes. The males have a glandular depression or a brood pouch on their belly for development of the eggs. The pouch (sometimes called a marsupium) is formed by two dermal folds protected by bony plates. During spawning the female transfers the eggs through her long ovipositor to the male's brood pouch. Most of the 50 species of pipefish currently known live in the sea. The southern Asian, Central and South American and African freshwater pipefish are thermophilous and in captivity require water temperatures between 22 and 28°C. They feed on plankton or on the fry of fish. Prey are sucked into the small, pipette-like mouth.

Bedotia geayi (308) lives in freshwaters of Madagascar and grows to a length of about 15 cm in the wild and 7—8 cm in captivity. It is a placid fish and is content in small aquariums. The male has a red margin around the caudal fin, whereas the margin of the female's caudal fin is translucent or milk-white. The breeding pairs spawn for several days in succession. The daily egg yield in the spawning season is very small. Each egg is provided with a thin filament and is suspended from an aquatic plant. The parents do not usually care for their eggs or fry. The free swimming young are big and greedily devour the nauplii of brine shrimp or *Cyclops*. Hard water, at least 10° dGH, is advisable for breeding this species.

308

Dwarf Rainbowfish or **Black-lined Rainbowfish** (309) is perhaps the most popular fish of the family Atherinidae kept in aquariums. In the wild it inhabits fresh waters of northern Australia in the vicinity of Cairns. The adult specimens are about 7 cm long. In the aquarium it is undemanding and feeds on any live food and is even content with dry and artificial food. Breeding is similar to that in the previous species. *Melanotaenia maccullochi* spawns in a single day. The fry hatch within seven to ten days at 25°C. One spawning yields up to 200 young. Only freshwater species of the family Atherinidae are kept in aquariums although most representatives of this family are sea fish. Recently some of the fresh water atherinids were ranged in an independent subfamily Melanotaeniinae.

Melanotaenia maccullochi

Melanotaenia maccullochi

278

310

Green Puffer-fish (310) is distributed in fresh, brackish and sea waters in southern India, the
Tetraodon fluviatilis Sunda Islands and the Philippines from where it is exported for use in
aquariums. It grows up to 17 cm long. The main food in captivity are
small aquatic snails and mussels. The male guards the eggs which are
laid on a stone and later he transfers the young to a pit in the sand. The
young are placid but the adults are aggressive. The body colour of the
Green Puffer-fish is very variable. Sexual distinctions are unknown.

Golden Puffer-fish (311, 312) lives in Thailand, Burma, the Malay Peninsula and perhaps also in
Chonerhinus naritus Sumatra and Borneo. It grows up to a length of about 30 cm. Golden
puffer-fish can be dangerous to people. In shoals, they attack people
who have fallen into water and bite pieces of flesh from their body.
The attacks are usually surprisingly quick and can be fatal. They have
a reputation similar to that of the South American freshwater piranha.
This fish is eaten by people in some regions of Burma. The fish are
caught with pieces of meat or small fish as bait. Young specimens
prosper in aquariums if 1—2 teaspoons of salt are added for every 10
litres of water. Water snails are accepted greedily. The best water temperature is from 22 to 26°C.

The body of the puffer-fish (Tetraodontidae) is usually bare, scale-

280

less, or covered with small bony plates. It has a large sac-like diverticulum of the gullet which can be distended with water or air. With the aid of this structure the fish can change its body shape into a spheroid (312). Most species live in tropical seas and only some inhabit the rivers of India and Africa. There are more than sixty species currently known to belong to this family. They devour any live food, including algae, corals, tunicates and sponges.

313

Three-spined Stickleback (313) lives in the waters along the European coast, in north-eastern Asia, Algeria, and North America. It grows to about 10 cm long and prefers to live in brackish water. The number of free spines before the dorsal fin and bony plates on the flanks varies with the salinity of the water. At spawning time the male builds a nest from plant material on the bottom where he spawns together with several females in succession. The brood number is 90 to 250 eggs. The young hatch within 10—14 days and the male undertakes the brood care.

Gasterosteus aculeatus

In the aquarium, the Three-spined Stickleback should be overwintered at low temperatures if possible. The summer temperature should also be low (22°C at the most). Live food such as zooplankton, worms and larvae of chironomid midges should be provided. In its natural habitat it also eats fish fry. The male guards the progeny very energet-

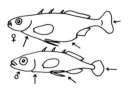

Gasterosteus aculeatus

282

314

ically, even attacking feet in the wild or hands in the aquarium if they get close to the nest or shoal of young.

The stickleback family (Gasterosteidae) comprises five genera. Three of them represent marine dwellers and two live in fresh water. They are too small to be of any real commercial importance, but in some places (e.g. in Finland) people give them to poultry.

Knight Goby (314) is one of the few freshwater representatives of the gobies (Gobiidae). It is *Stigmatogobius* distributed in southern Asia, the Greater Sunda Islands and the Philip-*sadanundio* pines. It grows to 8 cm long. All gobies have fused pelvic fins, forming a basin-shaped sucker which enables the fish to attach themselves to a firm substrate.

Almost all the fish of this family deposit their eggs on stones, with

283

315

a special preference for crevices. The eggs adhere very firmly to the substrate. The males guard the eggs and young. Sea salt should be added to the water, the concentration depending on the origin of the fish. Gobies feed on plankton, larvae of chironomid midges, fish meat, lamellibranchs and algae. Large species are very voracious.

Mud-rill Skipper (315) comes from the coasts of India, China and Bengal and, as reported by *Parapocryptes* Herre, it probably also lives in the Philippines. This species belongs to *serperaster* the family Apocrypteidae, which represents a transition between the gobies (Gobiidae) and the mudskippers (Periophthalmidae). The eyes of Gobiidae are below the level of the upper contour line of the head whereas the eyes of Periophthalmidae protrude above the head. At low tide the Mud-rill Skipper stays in depressions in the mud where it probably catches insects. In the aquarium it lives near the water bed. By night it is more lively and seeks any live food. The belly of the fish is a beautiful salmon red; the caudal fin is greenish with a yellow margin.

Chapter 9

BEAUTIES OF THE SOUTHERN SEAS

Aquarium culture of sea fish is a relatively new branch in the world of aquaristics. Of the sea organisms, invertebrates are more easily kept than fish. The main problem of keeping sea fish is their reluctance to reproduce in captivity; if they do reproduce, the young are very seldom reared. The other problems of marine aquaristics are the difficulties associated with growing sea plants (consumers of nitrogen compounds accumulating in the tank), the difficulty of providing suitable food substitutes for the fish since many species require a specific kind of food in nature, and the need for maintaining water purity. The water needs regular replacement with preparations of salt mixtures. Marine aquaria usually depend on continued imports of most species.

This last, brief chapter is not intended to give the reader a complete picture of the splendour and inexhaustible variety of the colour and form of sea fish. The aim is to use several examples to attract the reader's attention to the interesting aspects of those species which can be captured by the aquarium fish keeper in his travels. In this way the aquarist can avoid the great costs of expensive coral fish and the disappointment of possible failure to keep them alive. Apart from the delight of sea fishing the aquarist can learn about the natural habitat of the fish and employ this experience in preparing the aquarium to give the fish a chance to prosper. The species described in this chapter belong to various families and orders which will be briefly mentioned in the description of each species, since no general characteristics can be given.

Merou (316) (groupers, family Serranidae) is widely distributed in the Mediterranean and Adria-
Epinephelus guaza tic Sea, along the coast of west Africa and in the bay of Biscay. It inhabits rocky coastal waters up to depths of several hundred metres. The adult fishes are chestnut brown while the young are lighter in colour and covered with grey spots. Merous grow to a length of up to 140 cm. Young specimens are kept easily, soon become tame and will take food from the hand. The aquarium must provide rocky hiding places for this fish. It cannot be kept in small tanks for long because its growth is very rapid; however, it makes a good showpiece for public aquariums.

316

Brown Gaper (317) is a common species of the Mediterranean Sea and the Atlantic. It grows up
Serranellus hepatus   to a length of about 15 cm. This is the smallest representative of the
family Serranidae and inhabits the rocky and sandy coastal waters as
well as sea meadows with beds of aquatic plants of the genus *Zostera*.
It is most frequently encountered in waters deeper than 10 metres. In
summer it can be seen very close to the coast, 2—3 meters under the
water surface. It is a hermaphroditic species; the glands of both sexes
develop simultaneously in each fish. Hence each fish is capable of fertilizing itself. Its spawning time is June and July. It is very suitable for
domestic aquariums and is undemanding, slow and very inquisitive. It
devours water crustaceans, the meat of swan mussels, lean poultry
meat and so on. It should be fed moderately since it is very voracious.

Green-eyed Wrasse (318) is a common inhabitant of quays and of beds of the plants *Cystoseira*
Crenilabrus ocellatus   and *Zostera*. It lives in the coastal waters of the Mediterranean and
Adriatic Seas and in the Atlantic, in depths from 0.5 metres. The male
grows to 12 cm long; the female only 6 cm. During the spawning season from May to August, the male gradually builds several nests from
the fine filaments of algae, particularly of the genus *Cladophora*.
However, if this is not available, almost any other red, green or brown
seaweed will serve just as well. The dish-shaped nest is the size of
a plate and is built on the bottom. Young males up to the size of 7—
9 cm do not build nests. Females with ripe eggs wander along the coast
in shoals and spawn in the nests with both large and small males. If
rival males meet they take up a frontal posture and rapidly raise their

317

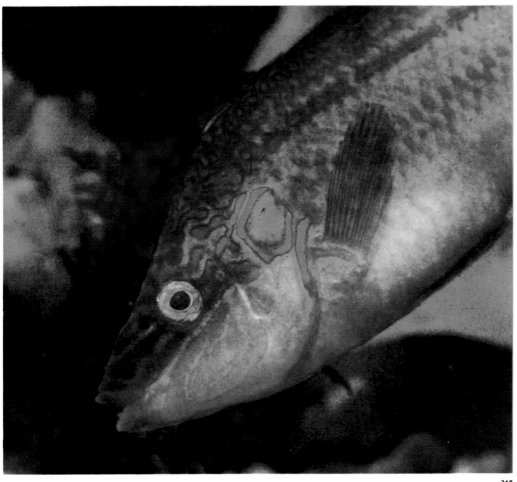

gill covers which are brilliantly coloured in the design of a peacock's eye. The larger males fan the eggs and fry in the nest by alternately moving the pectoral fins while adopting an oblique position with the head down. This species is suitable for the domestic aquarium. The water in the tank must be clean and well aerated. The fish needs both meat and vegetable food.

Mediterranean Wrasse *(Crenilabrus mediterraneus)* (wrasses, family Labridae) lives along the coast of the Mediterranean Sea near Portugal, the Azores and the western coast of Africa. The male is larger, growing to 17 cm long and is splendidly dark red or bluish. In May to June the pair builds a simple nest from a clump of algae at the border between the rocky and sandy bottom. The male spits sand into the nest; then the female deposits the eggs. The males are very aggressive and vigorously guard their residence. The fish of this species are very hardy and resistant in the aquarium. As they are voracious they demand a varied diet of meat.

319

Banded Sea-perch (319) inhabits the steep coasts of the Mediterranean, Adriatic and Black
Serranellus scriba   Seas, and the Atlantic. It often takes refuge in small caves among the
rocks. It grows up to 28 cm long. When attacking its prey it throws
itself up obliquely from the bottom. Like all fish of the genus *Serranellus* it is very inquisitive. The flesh is very tasty but full of tiny bones.
They are easily kept, particularly the younger specimens; their only
requirement is plenty of hiding places.

320

Peacock-wrasse (320) (wrasses, Labridae) commonly occurs ın the Mediterranean, Tyrian and *Crenilabrus pavo* Adriatic Seas and along the coast of Portugal. The male is larger than the female and grows up to 20 cm long. It keeps moving close to the bottom, taking sand into its mouth and chewing it and is usually followed by a shoal of *Crenilabrus ocellatus.* The robust males hunt near the rocky coast. They build small nests on rocks overgrown with algae and guard the eggs and fry. Small males spawn into the nests of the larger males; they do not guard the young but aggressively drive intruders out of their territory. In the aquarium this species soon loses its attractive colours.

The wrasses (family Labridae) are characterized by one dorsal fin whose spiny front part is much longer than the soft rear part. The scales covering their bodies are cycloid. Their teeth are sharp and line the jaws as well as the pharyngeal bones. The lips are thick and protractile. The family is known to contain more than 400 species which live mainly in tropical seas. A few species swim far north, up to the coast of Norway. Most of these northern species are small. A few wrasses however weigh 27 kg and more.

Outside the spawning season they associate in shoals and inhabit stands of algae and marine grasses. They feed on crustaceans, worms

321

and molluscs which they crush with their pharyngeal teeth. With their beautiful colours and small to medium size, they are popular aquarium species. Their meat is often very oily and of inferior taste.

Five-spot Wrasse (321) is widely distributed in the intertidal zone of the Mediterranean and
Crenilabrus Adriatic Seas. It often seeks refuge in rock crevices and in the stands of
quinquemaculatus seaweed of the genus *Cystoseira*. It grows up to 16 cm long.

The spawning season extends from April to June. The fish make a nest in the bottom sand or in a rock depression. The nest is provided with a large crescent-shaped front wall reinforced with red, green or brown algae or with small stones. The males stay at the same site for up to a year. The aquarium must be provided with plenty of hiding places among stones. The picture shows a female.

Its relative, the Ashy Wrasse *(Crenilabrus cinereus),* is a delicate species which is found in the Adriatic and Mediterranean Seas and in coastal waters of the Atlantic. It does not grow larger than 11 cm in length. The fish keep close to stands of sea plants such as *Zostera* and *Posidonia*. They spawn in May and June, in shallow waters at a depth of 50—70 cm. They make a furrow about as long as their body in the sand and reinforce its front wall with seaweed of the genus *Cladophora* and spat sand. They literally lie on the brood with their heads turned up and bravely drive away all intruders, however large they may be.

Doederlein's Wrasse (322) is the smallest species of the genus *Crenilabrus;* it is found in the
Crenilabrus Mediterranean and Adriatic Seas but nowhere is it common. It grows
doederleini only to 10 cm long. It lives mainly among vegetation, especially in
meadows of sea-grass *(Zostera marina)*. The male is red or orange with
a broad brown longitudinal band on the flanks with a silver band un-
derneath. The females are green. It is the least voracious species of the
genus *Crenilabrus.* It is shy and likes to hide in the stands of plants or in
narrow cracks in rocks.

The Black-tail Wrasse *(Symphodus melanocercus)* lives in the Mediterranean and Adriatic Seas. It lives in the densely vegetated littoral
zone where it occurs in large populations. Quays are also a favoured
habitat. It has an elongated body which grows up to 14 cm long. Young
specimens are perhaps the only real 'cleaners' in the seas where they
live. They remove the dermal parasites from other wrasses (Labridae)
as well as from groupers (Serranidae) and porgies or sea breams (Spa-
ridae). The fish that wants to be cleaned usually takes up an unusual
vertical, head-up position, signalling its readiness for cleaning. However, *Symphodus melanocercus* does not only live on parasites. In the
aquarium it will take the meat of molluscs, shellfish, crawfish and
pieces of fish or even lean poultry meat.

322

323

Blue-grey Wrasse (323) (family Labridae), is a common fish of the Indian and Pacific Oceans.
Coris formosa   The young individuals differ in colour from the adults. The ground
colour of a young *C. formosa* is almost the same as that of the related
species *C. gaimard.* In both, a red to brown colour prevails and is
interrupted by transverse and wedge-shaped white spots surrounded by
a darker shade. The adult specimens of both species are up to 40 cm
long. In adult *C. formosa* the ground colour is grey-blue with small
black spots; the throat is violet and the part of the head in front of the
broad, oblique, blue-white band under the eye is yellow to orange. The
end of the caudal fin and the margin of the anal fin are bluish.

Both species can be kept in the aquarium for a long time without
much difficulty. They need a sandy bottom in which they can bury
themselves for the night. Individuals should be kept separately since
the adolescent fish are quarrelsome. The diet should vary, with a preva-
lence of live food. These fish do not do well fed permanently on dry or
frozen food or food substitutes.

Moon Wrasse (324) is a native of the Indo-Pacific region and the Red Sea, where it lives in
Thalassoma lunare coral reefs. Its ground colour is an irridescent green with a purple-red
pattern on the head, body and fins. The male is larger than the female
and grows to about 30 cm long. The Moon Wrasse frequently spawns
in a shoal in which the fish swim close to the bottom, then turn up to
the surface where they change direction abruptly and return to the
bottom. The spawning act takes place during the abrupt turning just
below the water surface. One male often spawns with several females
at the same time. The eggs, which become veiled in a cloud of milt, rise
to the surface. This species is easy to keep in the aquarium. It is lively
and always hungry. The older the fish the more space they need; however, they are peaceable and not choosy about their food. In their natural habitat they feed on various invertebrates. In the aquarium they eat
meat of any kind and pieces of frozen fish meat, beef heart and brine
shrimp can be offered.

293

Bluehead (325, 326) is a common fish of the Caribbean Sea, near Bermuda, southern Florida
Thalassoma and the southern part of the Gulf of Mexico. It grows to a length of
bifasciatum about 14 cm. The youngest specimens are either whitish or yellow, with
a black longitudinal band on the flanks. The band disappears with age
and the body colour of the fish changes to canary yellow. At this colour
stage (at a length of about 4 cm) the fish are mature and the males and
females take on the same colour (325). Only the males then continue to
grow and change colour. Their head becomes blue and the body green,
with two transverse bars behind the pectoral fins (326). Young Blue-
heads usually clean the skin of other fishes by removing parasites from
them. They are attractive components of the aquarium, greedily taking
food such as frozen brine shrimp and pieces of meat, as well as dried
food.

Four-blue-streak Cleanerfish (327) is a typical cleaner which is endemic to the Red Sea. It
Labaricus grows up to a length of about 12 cm. Its body is torpedo-shaped and
quadrilineatus most locomotory thrust is provided by the pectoral fins, giving the fish
its characteristic swinging movement which probably signals that the
fish is ready to offer a 'cleaning service'. The ground colour is blue-
black with brilliant blue longitudinal bands. Like the Blue Streak *(Labroides dimidiatus)*, the fish of this species run a 'cleaning shop' in certain places among coral cliffs. They are visited by sick fish at certain
hours of the day which patiently queue for their turn. *Labroides dimidiatus* and *Labaricus quadrilineatus*, like other cleaner wrasses, clean

326

327

the body surface of other fish, but they also pick parasites from the mouths and gills through the raised gill covers of larger fish. The parasites of larger fish form a major part of the diet of these two species which can therefore be successfully kept in aquariums only together with large fish species.

Edged Wrasse (328, 329) is native to the Red Sea and the Indian and Pacific Oceans. It grows to
Coris angulata   a length of 120 cm. Young specimens have characteristic yellow or orange-brown crescentic spots below the dorsal fin (329). Other black spots decorate the dorsal fin and these usually persist throughout the life of the fish.

Due to their size, only young specimens are kept in domestic aquariums. They have particular requirements regarding food quality and only live animal food should be given as frequently as possible. Young fish are continuously supplied to the aquaristic market.

Many authors have observed that like the true 'cleaners' of the gen-

328

329

era *Labroides* and *Labaricus, Coris angulata* also pick parasites from the bodies of the larger marine fish when kept in community tanks. It is not known for certain whether they are true 'cleaners' in their natural environment.

Rainbow Wrasse (330)
Coris julis

is found in the eastern Atlantic from Great Britain to the Guinea Bay and in the Mediterranean and Adriatic Seas. Formerly ichthyologists recodnized two species, *C. julis* and *C. giofredi*. However, it was later found that the 'giofredi' colouring is typical of the immature stage of *C. julis*. The younger fish are mainly females. After a short transitional period (330) they change their colouration and resemble the beautifully coloured males. The male grows to a length of 25 cm. It has an orange longitudinal stripe on the flanks. The back is usually blue-green and the front part of the body has blue stripes. The ground colour of the females is brown or olive brown with one yellow and two dark blue, red or black stripes on the flanks. It is interesting that the males are sexually most active in the transition between the female to male colour phase. As soon as they have taken on the beautiful colouring of the male, they fall into a sort of sexual senility. The Rainbow Wrasse is

297

multi-coloured. It keeps swimming throughout the day but buries itself in sand at night. The fish move to deeper waters in winter. In spring they migrate to the coastal waters where they spawn. The small eggs, 0.65 mm in diameter, float on a large round drop of oil. In the aquarium the Rainbow Wrasse cannot withstand excessively high temperatures; it prospers in water at 21−23°C. Individuals of this species are voracious and eat any meat, particularly freshwater molluscs, brine shrimps or pieces of fish meat. They are easily fed in the aquarium where they thrive and may live for a long time.

Fairy Basslet, Royal Gramma (331) (family Serranidae) is a common species in the Caribbean
Gramma Sea. It only grows to a length of 6 cm. In the wild it lives among coral
hemichrysos cliffs at depths of 4−6 metres. Whether it is kept alone or in a shoal, it always needs plenty of hiding places in the aquarium. Like the large

330

groupers it likes to stand guard in front of its 'home'. Each specimen inhabits a territory which it aggressively defends against other fish of its own kind. The water should be crystal clear and very warm, about 28°C. This fish is not very choosy about its food and can be given dry food for a short time. It is difficult to catch and therefore the supply to aquarists is limited.

Russet Squirrelfish (332) (family Holocentridae) occurs in the Caribbean Sea and is widely
Holocentrus rufus distributed along the coasts of Bermuda and Florida. It grows to a length of about 25 cm. The long swimbladder reaches up to the head while in other members of this family the swimbladder is situated below the spinal column in the body-cavity. *Holocentrus rufus* belongs to the common inhabitants of the coral cliffs. When kept in captivity the main requirement is water purity and sufficient aeration. The fish prefer small live and freeze-dried crustaceans.

298

332

Diadem Squirrelfish (333) (Holocentridae) is widely distributed in the Pacific and Indian
Adioryx Oceans. It is particularly common near Madagascar, India and China. It
(= Holocentrus) grows quickly both in the wild and in captivity and fully grown speci-
diadema mens are up to 20 cm long. It has a strongly developed spine on the
posterior margin of the gill cover and short spines in front of the
caudal fin. The stripes on its flanks are very variable in colour, from
deep blood red to a pale orange-red. The lips and snout are typically
red. In the wild this species is a nocturnal feeder and attacks any live
prey, including smaller fish. In the aquarium it likes dim or diffused

333

334

light. It eats any food offered, but has a special preference for live food. This fish thrives if kept only with fish on its own kind or its close relatives. Other, smaller fish are often badly wounded by its frequent attacks.

African Butterfly Fish (334) (Chaetodontidae) is a common species found along the coasts of
Chaetodon chrysurus Africa and in the central regions of the Indian Ocean to Sumatra. It only grows to 15 cm. It is a good aquarium species. It feeds well on frozen brine shrimp *(Artemia salina)* and the like.

335

Saddled Butterfly Fish (335) comes from the Indopacific region and grows to a length of 20 cm.
Chaetodon falcula Aquarists often fail to persuade it to eat frozen or dried food. However, once acclimatized they are very hardy in captivity and some of them may live a long time. They need many hiding places or at least some partially shaded sites.

Long-nosed Butterfly Fish (336) (Chaetodontidae) is a common coral fish of the Indopacific
Chelmon rostratus region. It grows to a length of about 17 cm. Success or failure to acclimatize this species always depends on the food. The fish has narrow protruding jaws and with these it picks food from the crevices of coral reefs. Plankton floating on the water surface is usually refused, but small pieces of mollusc or fish attached to the sharp twigs of corals may be offered. It will follow other fish which pick their food from the

338

bottom. This peaceful fish is particularly fond of swimming among branches of corals.

Half-masked Butterfly Fish (337) inhabits the Red Sea where it grows up to about 20 cm. It is
Chaetodon
semilarvatus a delightful and popular species for sea aquariums, but it is rarely imported. The most important thing is to acclimatize the fish to dried or frozen foods as soon as possible. Only such acclimatized specimens become tame and long-living inhabitants of the aquarium.

Flag or **Threadfin Butterfly Fish** (338) lives in the Pacific and Indian Oceans and in the Red
Chaetodon auriga Sea. Individuals from the coastal waters of Australia grow up to 20 cm long while those from Hawaii are only 14 cm long. They are one of the hardiest marine aquarium species. Within a few hours in a tank they adapt to the new environment and begin to take food. They are not

303

339

choosy; freeze-dried crustaceans are devoured as greedily as pieces of live food. The fish soon becomes very voracious and should regularly be given smaller but more frequent rations. Long starvation is harmful as overfeeding.

Four-eyed Butterfly Fish (339) is the commonest species of the genus and lives in the tropical *Chaetodon capistratus* parts of the Atlantic and in the Carribbean Sea. In the wild it likes to eat the tentacles of polychaete tubeworms and sea anemones. In captivity it should be possible to acclimatize it to other foods, preferably freeze-dried tubifex worms or brine shrimps, or even live worms. Unfortunately, some specimens do not adapt to the new food and die within eight to ten weeks. The fish is constantly supplied to the American market but less frequently imported to Europe.

Common Butterfly Fish (340) is a fish of the tropical part of the Indopacific. It grows up to 15 cm *Parachaetodon ocellatus* long. It adapts to aquarium life quickly and willingly takes food. It is thermophilous and likes temperatures of 25—28° C. The food should consist of brine shrimps, enchytraeids, shrimps and molluscs. The fish stays in the lower layers of water, close to the water bed. It is placid and avoids flights. Unlike the related species, it soon loses its shyness.

304

Emperor Butterfly Fish (341) lives in the coral reefs in the Red Sea and grows to a length of
Chaetodontoplus about 16 cm. Like all fish from this region, it is thermophilous and
mesoleucus thrives in a temperature of 28° C. It is easy to keep and soon begins to
take food such as pieces of various crustaceans (e.g. *Mysis* or shrimps)
and molluscs. It enjoys tubifex worms. Unfortunately, it is often unsociable and tends to harass other fish in the tank.

341

342

Poor Man's Moorish Idol (342) is a native of the Pacific and Indian Oceans and the Red Sea. It
Heniochus reaches a maximum length of about 25 cm. Fish of the genus *Henio-*
acuminatus *chus* associate in large shoals. They have conspicuous dark transverse
bars and yellow pectoral, dorsal and caudal fins. Young specimens have
11 to 13 spinous rays in the dorsal fin, with the fourth ray being produced as a filamentous process. *Heniochus acuminatus* is very hardy
and undemanding in the aquarium. It can be given practically any food
and sometimes takes in directly from the hands. It is very susceptible
to drugs containing copper. It is a very popular marine aquarium fish.

Scat or **Argus-fish** (343) (family Scatophagidae) inhabits the coastal waters of the tropical part
Scatophagus argus of the Indo-Pacific. When fully grown it is about 30 cm long. It lives in

306

sea, brackish and fresh water but the adult specimens thrive best in sea water. The generic name means excrement-eater and this is a reference to the fact that it often stays near sewage outlets. It is omnivorous and in the aquarium it will accept all kinds of live food, as well as algae, lettuce, spinach and soaked porridge oats. The mouth of this fish is small. It swims in a swaying style like the coral fish. Food is incompletely digested in its alimentary canal and in consequence, its excrement pollutes the water and forms a large amount of detritus which must be removed from the aquarium by constant filtration of the water. A sub-species of the Scat, the Red Argus *(Scatophagus argus rubrifrons)* has a red forehead. Young specimens are spotted and have vertical stripes whereas the adults are uniformly green or brown.

Two other species, *Scatophagus tetracanthus* and *Selenotoca multi-fasciata* (family Scatophagidae), are also imported from time to time. All require breeding temperatures between 20 and 28° C. The spawning habits are similar to those of the lithophilous cichlids. Young specimens retain a bony cuirass on the head and shoulders for a long time. All attempts to breed any of these fish in captivity have failed.

343

344

Thread-fish (344) is a species of the family Carangidae. It lives in the Pacific and Indian Oceans.
Alectis ciliaris It grows to about 30 cm. The young fish have extremely long, thread-like processes extending from the soft fin rays of the dorsal and anal fins, and similar processes may also extend from the pectoral fins. The processes are often longer than the body. As the fish gets older they become shorter through abrasion until they completely disappear. In the aquarium this fish is very active and aggressive. It swallows the food instantly at the surface. This implies that placid fishes cannot survive if kept together with the Thread-fish which, on the other hand, usually flourish in large aquariums.

Common Fingerfish (345) belongs to the family Monodactylidae and lives in the warm seas and
Monodactylus argenteus brackish waters of Africa, southern Asia and Australia. Some species of this family also enter rivers. They have large eyes and their bodies are deep and strongly compressed. The head and mouth are comparatively small. The pelvic fins are very small. The Fingerfish grows up to

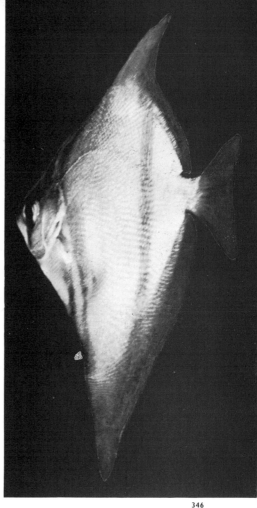

345

346

a length of about 23 cm. The first dorsal and anal fin rays are greatly extended and covered with scales. In the aquarium they soon get accustomed to brackish and fresh water.

Sebae Silverfish (346) is a relative of the Fingerfish and grows to about 20 cm long. It is found
Monodactylus sebae in the coastal and brackish waters of west Africa and sometimes swims up into the freshwaters of rivers. Despite its bizarre shape it has never enjoyed much popularity, perhaps because it has a rather dull colour. Most individuals of this and the previous species which are kept in aquariums remain shy. At higher temperatures (24—28° C) the Fingerfish and Silverfish thrive and may even become aggressive. They accept live food of all kinds; especially *Daphnia,* larvae of chironomid midges, tubifex worms, white worms *(Enchytraeus)* and similar food. They may be kept in fresh water for some time (up to a year) but brackish or sea water is closer to its natural environment. Successful reproduction in captivity has not been reported.

347

Clown Anemone Fish (347) belongs to the anemone fish family (Pomacentridae). This family
Amphiprion ocellaris comprises some 15 genera and almost 200 species. The genus *Amphiprion* itself contains 26 species. *Amphiprion ocellaris* is most widespread in the Indian Ocean and in the western parts of the Pacific. This beautifully coloured and popular fish grows up to 10 cm. It is not easy to keep in the aquarium. Like other anemone fish, it lives exclusively with the large anemone species. They can often be seen swimming among the stinging tentacles of sea-anemones *(Discosoma* and *Stoichactis)*. Like other fish, anemone fish are not immune to anemone poison, but apparently the anemone does not discharge its protective nematocysts towards these fish. In times of danger the anemone fish find refuge among the twigs of corals. The Clown Anemone Fish and some other anemone fish have been successfully reproduced in captivity. The eggs are laid and cared for on the stems of sea-anemones, hidden under the stinging tentacles.

Red Clown (348) lives in the Pacific and Atlantic Oceans and grows up to 14 cm long. Aquarists
Amphiprion frenatus claim that it is the hardiest of the anemone fish species and is the least dependent on sea-anemones. It has been successfully bred in captivity.

310

Gold-finned Clown (349) occurs widely in the Pacific and Indian Oceans and grows to 10 cm
Amphiprion sebae long. It is a close relative of the Saddle Back Clown *(A. polymnus)*; the two species differ only slightly. In the Saddle Back Clown the second white band of the adult never reaches down to the belly but remains in the dorsal fin as a saddle-shaped patch and just reaches to the middle dorsal part of the body. *A. sebae* is easily kept in aquariums, but it needs more care than *A. frenatus.*

The majority of the anemone fish are difficult to identify, since in many species the colours of the young specimens are almost identical. This is why some reference works often give different names to the same fish. An excellent description of the genus *Amphiprion* was pub-

351

lished in 1972 by G. R. Allen who studied the different developmental stages of all known species in nature, identified them exactly, and documented his work with many photographs and drawings.

Yellow-tailed Anemone Fish (350) is only known to live in the Indian Ocean; aquaristic litera-
Amphiprion
latifasciatus
ture usually refers to it as *Amphiprion xanthurus.* Fully grown specimens are up to 12 cm long. It is a hardy species in captivity. It swims among the stinging tentacles of sea-anemones and is not particular about the species of sea-anemone with which it lives.

White-tailed Damselfish (351) is a common fish of the Indo-Pacific and of the Red Sea. Parti-
Dascyllus aruanus
cularly large shoals of this species live off South Africa, India, Australia, China, and Melanesia. It grows up to about 8 cm long.

D. aruanus is frequently confused with the Black-tailed Humbug *(D. melanurus)* which has a broad black blotch on the caudal fin. *Dascyllus aruanus* is a very popular aquarium fish and is imported in large numbers, mainly from the Philippines and Ceylon. It is easy to keep in the domestic aquarium, despite the fact that it tends to be aggressive. This and other species of the genus *Dascyllus* are particularly suitable for beginners to keep in sea aquariums.

313

352

Three-spot Damselfish (352) occurs mainly in the Red Sea, off South Africa and in Polynesia. It
Dascyllus
trimaculatus
grows to 12 cm long. The adult individuals can easily be confused with the Hawaian species *D. albisella. D. albisella* has a single, large white blotch in the middle of the body. The young can very easily be dinstinguished because, apart from the blotch on the middle of the body, *D. trimaculatus* has another white spot on the front of the head. However, the blotches gradually disappear with age and the body colour of both species becomes uniformly dark. *D. trimaculatus* is a hardy species that feeds on small crustaceans which are picked out from the branches of corals among which they live. In its natural habitat the food consists of small shrimps and crab larvae. The fish also pick parasites from the bodies of other fish. In aquariums they greedily accept freeze-dried brine shrimps.

314

Marginate Damselfish (353) is widely distributed in the Red Sea and probably through the
Dascyllus marginatus   tropical latitudes of the Indo-Pacific. It grows to 8 cm long. Care and
breeding in the aquarium is simple and is much the same as in *Dascyllus trimaculatus*.

Lo-fox-fish (354) belongs to a family of rabbitfishes (Siganidae) which live in shoals in the
Lo vulpinus   Pacific Ocean. They are characterized by two spines in the pelvic fins,
one on either side, with three soft rays in between. They feed mainly on
algae. The common name of the family is derived from the fact that
they constantly twitch their upper lip like rabbits. *Lo vulpinus* is a very
popular aquarium fish. Some authors do not recognize *Lo* as a separate
genus (based mainly on the protruding jaws) and rank the species *vulpinus* directly under the genus *Siganus*. *Lo vulpinus* is a coral fish and

315

often hides among the branches of corals. It needs a large aquarium because it grows to a length of 24 cm. Once accustomed to replacer foods, the fish soon acclimatizes. Plants and algae must always be added to its regular diet. The fin spines are provided with poisonous glands and therefore the fish should be handled with care.

The fish of the related genus *Siganus* are deep bodied; their mouth is small, and their unpaired fins bear many spines inserted in a pit. *Siganus virgatus* (incorrectly called *S. vermiculatus* by aquarists) is a native of the Indian Ocean and is sometimes kept in aquariums. It grows up to 40 cm long. Besides algae, it feeds on various animal foods, such as molluscs and various marine crustaceans (*Mysis* and the like).

Polkadot Grouper (355) is a species of the family Serranidae. It is widely distributed in the
Chromileptes altivelis Indo-Australian region. It grows to 50 cm long. Young specimens have a small number of large dark blotches on the head, body and fins. With advancing age the number of the blotches increases, but their size diminishes. *Chromileptes altivelis* makes a beautiful showpiece since it likes to swim through the open spaces of the aquarium, unlike the other fishes of the genus which stay in hiding places. It is best fed with live food, but food replacers may also be supplied from time to time (freeze-dried brine shrimps or frozen fish meat). Some individuals remain shy, hide in the corners of the tank and are reluctant to accept food replacers.

Sergeant Major (356) (family Pomatocentridae) inhabits all tropical waters of the Atlantic,
Abudefduf saxatilis Pacific and Indian Oceans. It grows to 18 cm long. It is omnivorous and feeds on sea-anemones (mainly the genus *Zoantus*), algae on the bottom, crustaceans and pelagic tunicates, small fish, the larvae of various invertebrates, and adult molluscs (Nudibranchia). Shoals of these fish often filter the zooplankton. When danger threatens the fish quickly disappear among the coral reefs. The males are a splendid blue. They undertake the care of the deep red eggs. Young specimens are comparatively placid in the aquarium but older fish are very aggressive.

354

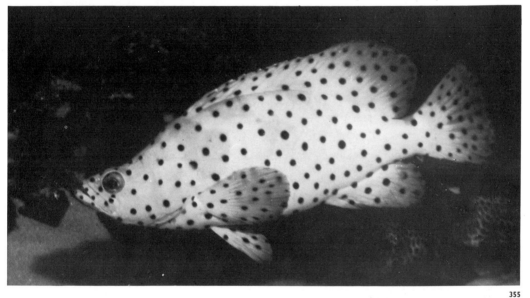

355

356

Neon Devil (357) lives in the Indo-Australian region of the Pacific. It grows up to a length of
Abudefduf oxyodon 10 cm. It can be acclimatized to food replacers but the aquarist often
faces other problems when keeping this species. Despite its small size it
is very aggressive and is also susceptible to various diseases which can
be fatal.

Blue Devil (358) lives in the southern parts of the Pacific and Indian Oceans and in the Red Sea.
Pomacentrus It associates in shoals over coral reefs. The eggs are deposited on
caeruleus filamentous algae. The male guards the brood for three to four days. In
the aquarium fish of this species readily accept live and dry food substitutes. They are often quarrelsome.

Orange Reef Fish (359, 360) is a native of the Pacific and Indian Oceans and grows to a length
Chromis xanthurus of 15 cm. The young are blue and their caudal fin is yellow. With increasing age the blue colour becomes darker and duller, but the bright yellow colour of the caudal fin is retained. Life habits of *Chromis xanthurus* are the same as that of *Pomacentrus caeruleus*.

Six-line Grouper (361) lives in the tropical zone of the Pacific and Indian Oceans. It grows to
Grammistes 25 cm. It has highly variable colouring. The adults are dark brown to
sexlineatus black, with white to cream yellow stripes along the flanks. The young have rows of flecks of varying size, or interrupted lines on their bodies. Fish 3 cm long have three such rows, fish 5 cm long four, and fish about 6 cm in length have six rows. Specimens 11 cm long have 11—12 rows

360

of flecks. Later the number of rows may decrease but they become wider.

The Six-line Grouper lives around coral reefs either alone or in small groups of two or three. In its natural habitat it is more active by night and hides during the day. The fish is considered to be the 'skunk' of coral reefs. In captivity it is not choosy about its food and swallows practically anything it sees in front of its mouth. The Six-line Grouper can only be kept with larger fish. Smaller individuals always risk being swallowed by their larger siblings. Care must be exercised when the fish is taken out of the aquarium because the inhabitants of the tank have often been observed to die suddenly. This is because the Six-line Grouper exudes a toxic secretion when it is frightened.

361

Speckled Angelfish (362) belongs to the family Pomacanthidae. It is native to the Red Sea and
Pomacanthus grows to a length of 40 cm. The distinctive feature of the species is
maculosus a transverse, crescent design in the middle of its body. It acclimatizes
easily in the aquarium and remains in good condition for a long time.
The food should contain vegetable supplements. Aquarists sometimes
confuse it with *Arusetta asfur* (see page 327).

362

363

Emperor Angelfish (363, 364) lives in the Indian Ocean and southwards to Madagascar. It
Pomacanthodes grows to 40 cm in length. This species also belongs to the family Poma-
imperator canthidae. The members of this family differ from the butterfly-fish
(Chaetodontidae) as they have a strong spine on the lower part of the
gill cover. Some species stay in pairs while others prefer solitude. It is
certainly the most splendidly coloured species of tropical seas. In many
pomacanthid species the colours change several times throughout their
life. They swim in a characteristic interrupted movement. The Emperor

364

Angelfish finds its food on corals and stones. It often keeps close to small caves in which it hides from danger. If disturbed it can produce clapping sounds which are clearly audible under water. All angelfish must be given vegetable supplements (preferably lettuce) to their regular food. Some of them are very sensitive and reluctant to accept food replacers.

The young of the Emperor Angelfish are deep blue with many concentric white rings on the body (363) and a complex pattern on the fins which changes with age. The colour keeps changing until the fish are mature. The adults (364) are reddish to purple and have 20 to 28 yellow horizontal stripes which run from the head to the base of the orange caudal fin. The Emperor Angelfish readily allows itself to be freed of parasites by the cleaner fish, *Labroides dimidiatus*. In the aquarium it requires a water temperature of 25° C. It will readily accept replacer foods.

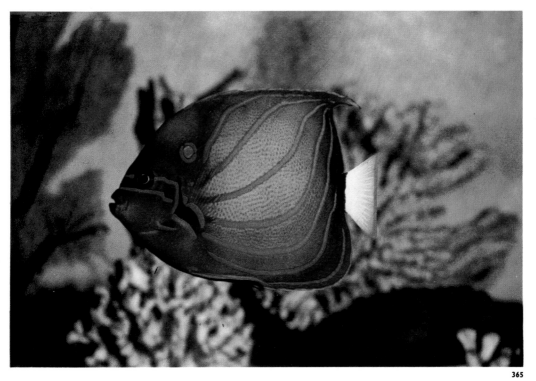

365

Ringed Emperor Angelfish or **Blue King Angelfish** (365) is widely distributed in the Pacific
Pomacanthodes and Indian Oceans, particularly off the coasts of Australia, India and
annularis Ceylon. In the neighbourhood of Ceylon it also inhabits turbid waters. In this area the young emerge in January, which is the warmest season of the year. At this time they can be captured easily. The adults are very hard to catch since they hide among corals during the day. Fishing is most likely to be successful on moonlit nights when the Ringed Emperor Angelfish rest on rocks as if asleep. They can be easily caught in

323

small nets since they appear to be transfixed by the light from a lantern.

The colouring is a beautiful bronze with blue stripes on the head, body and fins, and with a striking blue ring on the body behind the head. The caudal and pectoral fins are yellow to white. Sexual maturity is reached at a length of 15—30 cm. Like the preceding species, the Ringed Emperor Angelfish changes its colour at maturity. Requirements for care and breeding are the same as those for the Emperor Angelfish.

Blue Tang (366) belongs to the family of surgeonfishes (Acanthuridae) which live in tropical
Acanthurus
coeruleus
seas. On both sides of the caudal peduncle they have sharp protrusible spines used in fighting with other fish, usually of the same species. At spawning time they often associate in large shoals, swim to the water surface, eject the milt and eggs and dive again into the depths. Some species grow up to 50 cm long. The family comprises more than 50 species and many of them are splendidly coloured. *Acanthurus coeruleus* lives in the Caribbean and grows to a length of 34 cm. Until the age of about seven to eight months it is a dirty yellow-brown and sometimes orange. Later its ground colour changes into red-brown with blue areas. The belly, eye and lips are brilliant blue, the pectoral fins and the caudal fins yellow and the dorsal fin a dull yellow-green. In old fish a blue colour prevails. The aquarium in which these fish are to be kept should contain plenty of green algae to encourage the imported fish to acclimatize. Acclimatized specimens will survive happily in captivity for several years.

White-throated Surgeonfish (367) is found in the Indian and Pacific Oceans, the coastal
Acanthurus
leucosternon
waters of eastern Africa and the Comoro Islands. The African populations differ from those of the Pacific. Owing to its beautiful colours it is very popular among aquarists. It is an omnivorous species but vegetable food is preferred to animal food. It requires a rather high water temperature of 25—28°C. The fish is not very common in the wild. The success or failure of keeping it in the aquarium is believed to depend on the origin of the population imported. Fish from shallow waters adapt to the conditions of the aquarium much more readily than those from deep water.

Bahamian Surgeon (368) lives around the Bahama and Bermuda Islands and in the Mexican
Acanthurus
bahianus
Bay southwards to the coast of Brazil. The photograph shows the fish in its natural environment in the coastal waters of Cuba. *Acanthurus bahianus* stays near the bottom, in areas overgrown with plants. It feeds mainly on algae. It resembles *Acanthurus coeruleus*. It is only rarely imported to Europe.

324

366

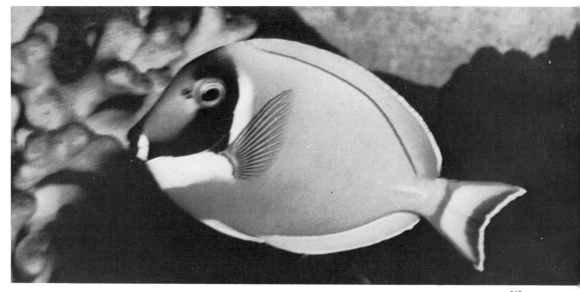

367
368

369

370

Flag-tail Surgeonfish (369) is a very brightly coloured fish of the Indian and Pacific Oceans. It
Paracanthurus grows to about 25 cm long and lives mainly off the coast of Ceylon. In
hepatus the aquarium it needs a water temperature between 25 and 30°C. Besides algae, it accepts molluscs, tubificid and white worms or crustaceans.

Red-toothed Filefish (370) is a common species of the Indian and Pacific Oceans and one of the
Odonus niger most frequently kept aquarium species of all triggerfishes (Balistidae).
It is placid and tame and will accept meat from the hand. The teeth are
orange to red.

Half-moon Angelfish (371) (family Pomacanthidae) comes from the Red Sea and grows to
Arusetta asfur a length of about 16 cm. It acclimatizes readily in the aquarium and can
live for a long time. Supplementary vegetable food is gratefully accepted by this species.

327

372

Yellow-faced Angelfish (372) is a splendid fish of the Indo-Pacific region. It grows up to 40 cm
Arusetta long. Fish of this species are very sensitive and very difficult to keep.
(= Euxiphipops) They need high quality live food and the sea water must have a con-
xanthometopon stant pH value. The water must not be too fresh and its nitrite content
must be kept very low. If it is cared for by an experienced aquarist, it
can survive for a long time.

Rock Beauty (373) comes from the Caribbean. It grows to 60 cm long. There are marked
Apolemichthys differences between the young and the adult specimens. The ground
(= Holacanthus) colour of the young is yellow with a dark, blue-ringed blotch on the
tricolor back. The adults are orange-yellow and their flanks are velvet black.
The dorsal and anal fins have black borders. In the aquarium it thrives
at water temperatures of about 25°C. This greedy species is not choosy
about its food. The fish are very susceptible to infestation with parasitic
fungi and are particularly susceptible when transferred to another tank,
or when the water in the tank is abruptly replaced. Besides animal food
it needs vegetable supplements, e. g. thoroughly washed lettuce leaves.

Black-and-gold or **Two-coloured Angelfish** (374) occurs in the waters of the Indo-Pacific
Centropyge bicolor region and does not usually grow longer than 10 cm. It prospers best in
an aquarium overgrown with filamentous algae. It is inquisitive rather
than shy. Food should be given in small amounts throughout the day.
Overfeeding in large single doses is harmful to the fish.

Sharp-nosed Puffer or **Ocellated Toby** (375) is a common species of the Pacific and Indian
Canthigaster solandri Oceans and the Red Sea. It belongs to the family of tobies (Canthigas-
teridae). Its eyes move independently of one another. The fish of this
species are extremely inquisitive creatures. Like all tobies and the puf-
fer-fishes to which they are closely related, they eat snails and any live
or dead meat they happen to find in the aquarium. In this way they

328

keep the water of the aquarium clean and free from pollution. Frozen and dried food, such as brine shrimps and tubifex worms, is also accepted.

Black-spotted Puffer (376) is an inhabitant of the Indian Ocean and is found from South Africa *Arothron* to Polynesia. Around the Seychelles they grow to 35 cm long, while *nigropunctatus* those captured farther to the east are probably somewhat smaller. It is

374

remarkable in the aquarium for its lemon yellow colour with irregularly distributed tiny black dots. Its teeth are white. It likes to feed on live corals and accepts food replacers with reluctance.

White-spotted Blowfish (377) is a native of the waters around the Seychelles and many other
Arothron hispidus places in the Indian and Pacific Ocean. It grows to about 50 cm long. At the base of the pectoral fins and gill openings (clefts) the fish bears a yellow ovoid pattern with a pale ring-like rim. The body colours of the young are more pronounced than those of the adults. Their favourite food consists of marine crustaceans. In captivity they will also take molluscs and other animal food. It likes to hide in corals or under stones.

Black Filefish (378) (family Balistidae) comes from the Indo-Pacific region and grows to
Melichthys ringens a length of about 50 cm. The ground colour of the body is very variable; some of the colours seen are light beige, green, red-brown and

375

deep black. This fish likes to sleep lying on its side, as if it were dead. It has sharp teeth with which it captures and crushes crabs and sea urchins (echinoderms). It easily adapts to aquarium conditions and is very hardy. The stock of a community tank must be carefully chosen because the Black Filefish is pugnacious and quarrelsome.

378

Whitefin Lion Fish (379) belongs to the family of scorpion fish (Scorpaenidae) which have
Pterois radiata poisonous glands at the base of fin rays and near the spines on the head. *Pterois radiata* is a spectacularly coloured species of tropical fish which is popular among aquarists. It lives in the Indian and Pacific Oceans and in the Red Sea. It grows to 20 cm. Small shoals of these fish seek dark hollows where they spend most of their time. They have no natural enemies. Larger specimens are cannibals which often swallow smaller fish of their own kind.

Although *Pterois radiata* is a nocturnal fish it can easily acclimatize to day activity. It does not like picking food from the bottom, but prefers pieces of ox heart, fish or mollusc, liver and so on. This is best left floating on a loop of thread in the water. The fish will soon help itself. It is advisable not to overfeed but instead to offer food twice or three times a week. They like to eat live freshwater fish.

Fight Firefish (380) is closely related, if not identical, to the Red Firefish *(Pterois volitans),*
Pterois miles which lives in the Red Sea, near South Africa and Polynesia. It grows up to a length of 25—35 cm. Its body is covered with wide alternating dark and light transverse bands. The membranes in the dorsal fin and in the pectoral fins develop into fan-like projections. Care in the aquarium is the same as for *Pterois radiata* (above).

332

381

Snakehead Goby (381) belongs to the family of gobies (Gobiidae) whose pelvic fins are fused, *Gobius ophiocephalus* or at least partially fused, to form a sucking disc. The family includes many small tropical species which live in the surf zone. *Gobius ophiocephalus* occurs mainly in the Mediterranean and Adriatic Seas. It grows up to 10 cm long. It likes to live among *Zostera* beds. Adults spawn from March to May. The species adapts easily to aquarium conditions and greedily takes various animal foods.

Bucchichi's or **Striped Goby** (382) occurs in the surf zone of the Mediterranean and Adriatic *Gobius bucchichii* Seas. It is also frequently found in harbours. The fish always keeps close to the sea-anemone *Anemonia sulcata*. The mucus film on their bodies protects them against the stinging tentacles of *Anemonia sulcata,* but not, however, against other sea-anemone species. The fish is not

382

383

completely dependent on the anemones; it only seeks refuge among their tentacles when in danger. Crustaceans and pieces of meat are the best food for this species.

Tentacle Blenny (383) *Parablennius tentacularis* belongs to the family of the blennies (Blenniidae) which live in the coastal zones of all temperate and tropical seas. Some species also live in brackish waters, while others are found in fresh waters. A revision of the tribe Blenniini was published in 1977 by H. Bath. According to this work, the tribe has 15 genera and 70 species are used here.

Parablennius tentacularis occurs commonly in the Mediterranean and Adriatic Seas where it lives in stone crevices and among rocks overgrown with plants of the genus *Posidonia.* In their natural habitat the males form and defend their own territories and take care of the

335

384

385

brood. In the aquarium this fish must have plenty of hiding places, some of which can be chosen by the male and protected against all rivals. If there is a shortage of hiding places the males soon kill one another. *Parablennius tentacularis* grows to a length of about 15 cm.

Capuchin Blenny (384) lives in the Mediterranean Sea, off the coast of North Africa, in the *Coryphoblennius* Atlantic Ocean and in the English Channel up to the North Sea. It stays *galerita* in the fissures and cracks in rocks or under stones. It rides the surf and often jumps onto land where it seeks food, such as *Chthalamus stellatus*. It grows to about 7 cm. The water in the aquarium must be rich in oxygen.

An even smaller fish of this family, the Adrian Blenny *(Lipophrys adriaticus),* is a native of the Adriatic and Mediterranean Seas. It seeks refuge in the holes left by the burrowing bivalve *Pholas dactylus* at the low-tide mark. Individuals of this species do not grow longer than 5 cm. The males stay in the holes with only their heads sticking out while protecting the brood. They leave the hiding place to seek food in early morning and late evening when the tide is high.

Another very small representative of the family is the Dalmatian Blenny *(Lipophrys dalmatinus)* which only grows to 4 cm long. Habits and distribution are the same as in *L. adriaticus.* The heads of the males are bright yellow and may be seen sticking out of holes. The aquarium in which this species is to be kept can be small but must have narrow hiding places. The fish eats crustaceans, worms and pieces of molluscs.

Bloodthirsty Blenny (385) is a common fish of the Black, Adriatic and Mediterranean Seas and *Pictiblennius* the Atlantic Ocean. It grows to about 20 cm long. It differs from other *sanguinolentus* blennies by swimming freely close to the bottom. It is very shy and often changes its hiding place. Spawning time is from April to August. The male protects a large brood (3,000 — 12,000 eggs) under a stone or in a crack among stones. Its ground colour is olive green, yellowish or sometimes brown, depending mainly on the colour of the substrate on which the fish lives. The rims of the pectoral fins bear red spots. Another species, the Tompot Blenny *(Parablennius gattorugine),* is still larger (20 — 25 cm long) and has huge tentacles branched like a tree. The meat of all blennies is very tasty and in some countries is also very popular.

Darkstriped Blenny *(Parablennius rouxi)* inhabits the rocky coastal waters of the Adriatic and Mediterranean Seas. It stays on rounded stones in water which reaches a depth of about 25 metres. In recent years large shoals of this fish have been observed close to the outlets of city sewage canals from the town of Komiža, on the island of Vis. *Parablennius rouxi* grows to 7 cm long. The male is larger and more robust than the female. On the front part of the dorsal fin the male has a brilliant blue oval 'mirror' and the tentacles above the eyes are larger than the female's. In the aquarium this fish needs special care; the water should be rich in oxygen and the temperature should be kept low.

Zvonimir's Blenny *(Pictiblennius zvonimiri)* occurs in abundance in the rocky coastal waters of the Black, Mediterranean and Adriatic Seas where it lives in narrow crevices between stones and rocks, usually on the shaded sides of islands. The male is larger than the female and grows to a length of about 7 cm. His head is brown-red in colour. At spawning time he entices the female by swaying movements; then he leads her to his cave, while bending his body up and down. Fish of this species acclimatize easily in the aquarium. The main requirement is water purity.

Cat's Blenny (386) occurs sporadically in the waters along the Adriatic and Mediterranean
Lipophrys canevae coasts and usually keeps in groups below low tide level. It grows to 7 cm long. At spawning time, which extends from June to August, the fighting males are splendidly coloured. A male in spawning livery shows gill covers which are shining yellow to orange-red, has a blue to black forehead and dark grey cheeks. When they attack one another, they arch their backs. In courtship displays they raise the gill covers and when luring the female they jerk their heads and swim a zig-zag course to show the female the way.

Eyed Blenny (387) occurs abundantly in the Black, Adriatic and Mediterranean Seas. It grows to
Salaria pavo about 12 cm long. The male has a huge helmet-like hump on the head. The fish lives in hollows under stones. The eggs are deposited in crevices in rocks and are protected by the males. The eggs are never left, not even during low tide. This species is easily kept in the aquarium. It is important to provide plenty of hiding places for individual males. If the tank is small or if there are not enough hiding places the males will kill one another. *Salaria pavo* has been bred in captivity many times. It prospers in sea or brackish water.

Sphinx Blenny (388) lives in the Black, Adriatic and Mediterranean Seas. It grows to 8 cm long.
Aidablennius sphynx It is a splendid multi-coloured fish with a high dorsal fin. Spawning time

386

387

388

389

is May and June and the eggs are laid in small caves. The male removes all sand, algae, shells and so on, and carries this material in its mouth far away from the spawning place. The Sphinx Blenny always stays in the intertidal zone and does not leave the brood (provided it does not dry out), not even at low tide, or it returns immediately with the high tide. It has a very good sense of orientation; if removed 50 metres away from the nest, it finds it again within 24 hours. It adapts easily to aquarium conditions; it is very inquisitive and its favourite food consists of planktonic crustaceans as well as tubifex worms and small pieces of beef and lean poultry meat.

Shrimpfish (389) belongs to the family Centriscidae. Members of this family are distributed in
Aeoliscus strigatus   the Pacific and Indian Oceans. Their bodies are covered with bony
armour. The tail is reduced and the dorsal fin protrudes backwards and
forms a pointed end to the body. The fish of this family swim with their
heads pointing down and their tails up. Most of them associate in small
groups. In their natural habitat they live in association with sea-urchins
but the reason for this behaviour is still unknown. They acclimatize
quickly in the aquarium and readily take dried or frozen brine shrimps
which have been dipped in hot water to make them fall to the bottom.
Small pieces of meat or crustaceans are also eaten.

Sprightly Dragonet (390) is a brightly coloured representative of the family Callionymidae. It
Callionymus festivus   occurs in the Mediterranean, Adriatic and Black Seas. The male (390)
grows to 14 cm in length. It lives in a water depth of 1—3 metres and
moves by darting suddenly on the sandy bottom. The spawning time is
July to August. Females which are ready for spawning jerk their first
dorsal fin. During the spawning act the pair swim to the surface where
the fish eject their eggs and milt. Droplets of oil keep the eggs on the
surface. In captivity the fish needs well oxygenated water and feeds on
various kinds of animal food.

390

391

Tripterygium nasus (391) belongs to the family Tripterygiidae. Distinctive features are three dorsal fins and a comparatively small pointed mouth. It inhabits the intertidal zone but it can be found to a depth of 25 metres. Rocky places overgrown with thickets of various algae are its favourite environment. This species never seeks refuge, not even if pursued, but just 'skips' on the rocks when disturbed.

The male (391) is about 7 cm long and displays a splendidly red colour in the spawning season. The head, throat and pelvic fins are black. The females are smaller and are inconspicuously light brown in colour. The eggs are laid on bare walls of rocks. The male protects a territory around the brood of about 4 metres in diameter. *Tripterygium nasus* is a common fish which occurs everywhere in the Mediterranean and Adriatic Seas. In the aquarium it needs well-filtered and oxygenated water and its food should consist of small planktonic crustaceans such as *Cyclops* and *Daphnia*. These should be given in small but frequent doses. It is very sensitive to any turbidity of the water and often dies for no apparent reason.

Shore Clingfish (392, 393) belongs to the family of clingfishes (Gobiesocidae) which lack spines
Lepadogaster in the dorsal fin. On the ventral side of the body they have a sucking
lepadogaster disc (393), which is formed by the pelvic and the pectoral fins and also
by modified bones of the shoulder girdle. All species of this family are
small fish which live in the intertidal zone of coastal waters and hide
under stones. The sucking disc enables them to cling very firmly, even
to smooth rocks, and to withstand the pounding of even the strongest
waves. The fish of the genus *Lepadogaster* can be found on the European coasts of the Black, Adriatic and Mediterranean Seas and around
the coasts of Great Britain. The Shore Clingfish grows to 7—12 cm in
length. Adult specimens have a fringed skin fold above the nasal open-

393

ings. They are difficult to capture. It is often necessary to remove many stones from around the hiding place of the fish to get to the sandy bottom before working towards the centre to expose and catch it. It is advisable to put a stone on the net before inspecting it. The fish quickly moves on its sucking disc and tries to keep to the underside. This species is very resistant to the rigours of transportation. The Shore Clingfish is tolerant to other fish of the same species. They will live peacefully together among the stones scattered on the bed of the tank. They live on tubifex worms, larvae, or pupae of chironomid midges and pieces of fish and poultry meat. On one occasion five specimens were fed exclusively with lean pork for six months. They grew exceptionally well, even though this food is generally recognized as being completely unsuitable for fish. Only with great difficulty did they later acclimatize to a varied diet.

344

BIBLIOGRAPHY

Allen, G. R.: *The Anemonenfishes* (Their Classification and Biology). T. F. H. Publ. Inc., Neptune, New Jersey, 1972

Bath, H.: *Revision der Bleniini* (Pisces: Blenniidae). Senckerbergiana, Biologica, 57, 4/6, 167—234, 1977.

Dahlstrom, P., Schiotz, A.: *Aquarium Fishes.* Collins, 1972.

Emmens, C. W.: *How to Keep and Breed Tropical Fish.* T. F. H. Pubns, 1962.

Klausewitz, W., Peyronel, B., Tortonese, E., Vesco, V. D.: *Life in the Aquarium.* Octopus, 1974.

McInerny, D., Gerard, G.: *All About Tropical Fish.* Harrap, 1966.

Madsen, J. M.: *Aquarium Fishes in Colour.* Blandford, 1974.

Mayland, H. J.: *Complete Home Aquarium.* Ward Lock, 1976.

Sagar, K. (ed.): *World Encyclopedia of Tropical Fish.* Octopus, 1978.

Scheel, J.: *Rivulins of the Old World.* Publ., Inc., Jersey City 2, N. J., 1968.

Simister, W.: *Home Aquarium Book.* David and Charles, 1976.

Torchio, Menico: *World Beneath the Sea.* Orbis Pub., 1972.

Vevers, H. Gwynne: *Tropical Aquarium Fishes in Colour.* H. G. & G. Witherby, 1957.

Walker, Braz: *Marine Tropical Fish in Colour.* Blandford, 1975.

INDEX OF COMMON NAMES
(Bold figures refer to numbers of illustrations)

INDEX OF SCIENTIFIC NAMES
(Bold figures refer to numbers of illustrations)